SORAYA

RUNES

SORAYA

RUNES

GEDDES & GROSSET

Published 2007 by Geddes & Grosset
David Dale House
New Lanark, ML11 9DJ
Scotland

Text copyright © Soraya 2007

Artwork copyright © Martin Conway 2001

Layout and cover design copyright © Geddes & Grosset 2007

First printed 2007

ISBN 13: 978-1-84205-106-1

Printed and bound in Poland

Contents

Introduction

PEOPLE from every walk of life, the world over, are familiar with the use of symbols or signs in their communication. We have them on our roads telling us to slow down, speed up or stop. Supermarkets, oil companies, political parties, the Church and the medical profession, are among the many who use symbols to identify their organisations and the elements within them. Some symbols are modern, designed by graphic designers and artists in marketing companies; others are drawn from history and tradition. In this book we are going to study some very special symbols that come from ancient Nordic culture: the runes.

You may be surprised by just how familiar you are with some of these runes as many are in common use today. For example, in Scotland, most of us readily recognise the symbol used by the Scottish National Party, but their logo is in fact based on a runic symbol called *Othel* or *Othillo*, which can be interpreted to stand for home, family and integrity. When we cross our fingers to make a wish, we are making another symbol called *Geofu*, or *Gefu*, which represents harmony and togetherness.

Of all the esoteric disciplines that are used today, for me, the runes have proved themselves time and again to be among the most accurate of them all.

The first time that I heard of them, I was very curious about them and, being an avid numerologist, I started to work out the hidden influence in the word rune. The numerological value of *rune* is 22 and this number is associated with crossing a bridge. Quite apt really, since casting the runes will allow us to cross the bridge between the present and the future.

I was fascinated by these ancient inscriptions and wondered how they could help me in my life. Each night before I went to sleep I would draw one rune, asking as I did so, "What have I experienced today?" I put them in an onyx box and kept them beside my bed. It was not long before I realised how accurate they were. Later, I would draw another in the morning, asking what that day would have in store for me. In this way, I managed to take advantage of opportunities that were shown to me and to avoid some pitfalls too.

When you are using the runes for guidance, it is very important to think of one question only. Bear in mind, runes cannot answer an "either-way" question. You can ask, "What will be the result if I do this?" But you cannot ask, "Is it better to do this or that?" When you have prepared a single question in your mind, draw a rune from the box or bag where you keep them. If you want to ask a different question, you can make another draw, but you can do this no more than three times in any one day.

There are 25 runic symbols and each represents a letter of the Germanic alphabet. Each rune tells an historical story to help us to understand or deal with issues in our lives. Some runes, no matter which way they fall, look exactly the same.

An x, for example, looks the same whether it is the right way up or standing on its head, but other runes will give a more negative interpretation if they fall upside down or in the reverse position.

All those years ago, I was often wary of the symbol that I had chosen when I drew a rune and imagined the worst; I would be afraid that the predicted day's events would be disastrous. I remember on one particular occasion, I was lying in my bed thinking about what I had to do that day. I realised with delight that I had no appointments and no pressing responsibilities. With a smile on my face at the thought of a free day, I drew a rune from my box. But my smile soon disappeared when I saw that the symbol I had picked warned of sudden unexpected changes. I couldn't resist the temptation to draw another rune to try to find the influences surrounding these changes. This time I drew a one that depicted the home and matters connected to property. More panic! I was so concerned that something not very pleasant would happen that I was afraid to go out visiting or shopping.

Around noon, a large delivery van arrived with my new suite on board. I hadn't expected it to come for another two weeks, but here it was being delivered, and I hadn't made arrangements to have the old one uplifted. Luckily, a quick call to the local charity shop solved that problem and eventually I was able to put my house to rights with one – not two – suites and enjoy seeing my new furniture in my home. What I am really trying to say here is, when you use the runes, try not to imagine the worst as I did when I first began to use them. That day my runes gave me advance warning that something unexpected (not drastic) was about to happen that would affect my plans and be connected to my property.

A brief history of the runes

Runes have been around for centuries and there have been many variations over the years. The number of runes in the runic alphabet varied widely in different places and at different times. At one point they increased to 33, whilst to the other extreme there were as few as 16, but they have evolved to what we know and use today. Traditionally, runes were small pebbles or pieces of wood, 25 in all, and each one had a symbol inscribed on them. In addition, many people carved rune symbols onto their personal possessions, such as their weapons, bowls, or jewellery.

It is thought that runes originally derived from an Etruscan alphabet used by the Italic tribes of the Eastern Alps, and were developed by the Germanic peoples of Bohemia around the second to third centuries AD. The earliest surviving runic inscriptions date from the middle of the third century, though they were in wide use during the fourth to the eighth centuries. In the middle ages, the runes were used as an alternative alphabet to the standard Latin one.

In olden times, runes were used for divination and magick, but had to be used in secret. Anyone found using them could be banished, imprisoned or executed because of the power that they were believed to hold. Warriors would use runes to find out if they would come home safely and victorious from battle. Farmers would consult the runes on the best times to plant or harvest their crops. Combinations of runes were bound together to make a talisman for fertility, love, protection, or healing and sometimes to curse an enemy.

In Sweden, the rune Thorn or Thurizas is still used today in the modern Icelandic alphabet. Gradually, the runes were spread throughout Europe by the Anglo-Saxons.

The 25 basic runes are known as the Futhark. This is derived from the sounds of the first six letters, F-U-Th-A-R-K. Norse mythology speaks of Odin (Woden), the All-father sacrificing himself for the sake of knowledge. He hung from the tree of life by his ankles and lost or sacrificed his eye in order to drink from the well of Mimir, which bestowed great knowledge.

Using the runes

The ancient knowledge of the runes has been passed on to us to use for guidance and wisdom. Many feelings and situations are associated with each rune and it is important that you are familiar with them to fully understand and interpret them. You will find stories associated with each rune symbol on the following pages. These stories are based on my understanding, but when you begin to live with your runes, you will have different experiences of your own that you will attribute to each symbol. This will be your interpretation and this is what you should base your understanding on. Always remember to let your experience and your intuition be your guide.

Finding your runes

These days, it is not difficult to find rune shops that sell rune stones or cards. They can even be purchased on the internet, but by far the best way of getting your own set is by making them. The easiest way is to find 25 small flat stones of a similar size. I have found the best ones on beaches. Once you're happy with your collection, wash and dry them, then lay them out on a table or mat. Using this book, go to the section that shows you the rune shape and keep it handy for reference. You could set the atmosphere by lighting some candles and incense. As you sit there, handle each stone and allow its energy to tell you what rune it should identify with. Next, using the illustration in this book, mark the symbol on the chosen stone. Remember, one of the 25 stones, the "wyrd" rune, should be kept blank. You can mark your runes initially with a pencil and later, when you have marked them all, you can use paint. Then make or find a bag or box to keep them in. My rune box has treasured mementos in it too.

While you are in the mood, make a special cloth to lay your runes out on or to "cast" them, as it is commonly called. If you wish, draw symbols and shapes on your casting cloth. When all this is done, lay your stones out on a windowsill so that they will catch the rays of the sun in the daytime and the rays of the moon at night. Be patient and leave them on the windowsill for a full month, saying a little prayer of dedication to them each night or morning:

"Woden you who hung from the tree
Help me, please, the mysteries to see.

Be my guide each time I cast
That I may see present, future and past."

If you have purchased rune stones, you will need to
wash them before you lay them out on the sill. If you
decide to buy cards, these too should be laid out in the
same way, so that they become familiar with your
energy. Your runes are now ready to work with.

Understanding the runes

Part one

Keep your runes in their box or bag in your bedroom
by your bed. Each night ask the question: "What have
I learned or experienced today?" Choose one rune at
random and read the story in this book associated with
the rune that you have chosen. Try to apply the situation that the rune is describing to your own life, and
write that down in a notebook. Do this for at least one
month, or until you have experienced all the runes.
Once you have completed this exercise, you are ready
for part two.

Part two

Each morning, when you wake up and before you do anything else, ask yourself: "What will I learn or experience today?" Then choose one rune at random. This will be your first exercise in predicting coming events. Now refer to both your notes and the interpretation in this book. At the end of the day, write a description of the event or experience in your notebook.

When you want to be reminded what a rune means, look to your own notes first. Remember, your runes are in personal communication with you and your experience or interpretation may be different from anyone else's. When you have done these exercises, you should be familiar enough to understand the meaning of all your runes and be ready to work with them.

Working with runes

Working with runes can be as simple or as complicated as you wish to make it. You can ask one question and chose one, two or three runes or stones for your answer. You can carry out a complete Celtic or astrological spread for a complete reading and you can even make up your own spreads. You must, however, be completely focused. I have known situations whilst working for myself, when I have had several questions in mind but thought I was asking one particular question, only to have another answered. The best way to focus before asking questions is to set the mood before you begin.

Asking a question

When you are using the runes for guidance or to ask a question, it is very important to think of that question only. Make a list of your questions before you start then light a candle, incense, or both, and sit quietly with your rune cards or stones in front of you. I usually concentrate on my question whilst I am holding my runes or tumbling my stones in their bag. Using rune cards, I then spread them in a circle and, still thinking of my question, I choose one rune. If my answer is not clear I may choose one or two more to clarify, but never more than three altogether. When I am using my stones, I keep them all in their bag and, when I am ready, I put my hand into the bag and draw out one stone. Again, if I am not clear on the answer that I am being given, I will choose another one or two.

Runes cannot answer an "either-way" question, so you must be very clear in your mind. You can ask in the fashion of, "What will be the result if I do this?" But you cannot ask, "Is it better to do this or that?" I am sure that you will find, as I did, that the ancient runes, as well as being fascinating to work with and understand, are by far one of the most accurate disciplines available to us today.

Casting the runes

Remember that the runes are giving you guidance and you will be shown opportunities that you can take advantage of or obstacles that you can avoid. Once you are comfortable with the interpretations, you can begin to use the runes in many ways.

The Runes

1
The Story of Feoh

ONE of my regular clients, with whom I had become quite friendly, asked me to read the tarot cards for a woman and her daughter-in-law. She called to say that her sister and her nephew's wife were visiting from Manchester and that they had been having a really hard time recently. Would I do her a favour, and read for them to give them some guidance? I agreed to go and see them the following morning.

I was very embarrassed at the reading; there I was reading for the daughter-in-law who, according to my client, was experiencing a really hard time, and all I could see in the tarot was money, money, and more money. I told her everything that I could see and I

19

remember the expression on her face as she stared at me at the end of the reading. She looked as though I had been talking rubbish, making things up.

When we had finished, her mother-in-law came through. I prepared the cards for her reading and spread them out as usual. I looked at the cards with disbelief. They told almost the same story as the first reading had, money all through the cards, and wealth beyond the norm. I kept telling the woman that she had nothing to worry about. I told her that within three months she would be very wealthy and would buy a large house – a mansion – with another house in the grounds. There would be trees all around her new home and her whole life would change. During this time, there would be a new addition to the family. The woman thanked me as I took the tape from the tape recorder and handed it to her. I could tell that she hadn't believed a word I had said and that her thanks were only given out of politeness.

During my journey home, I kept going over and over the cards that had come out in both readings. I blamed myself because I hadn't really wanted to go and do this favour but had felt almost obliged to. Perhaps this was some sort of punishment for resenting the readings. Over the next few months, my friend called a few times. I asked if her family were keeping better and she assured me that they were just the same. I think she was just as embarrassed as I was by their readings. She told me that she had listened to their tape and that it all seemed a bit far-fetched.

One Saturday evening, 12 weeks after their reading, I was sitting at home when my phone went. It was the lady from Manchester.

"I had to call you," she said. "Something amazing has happened."

I told her to calm down, as she was really excited, and I asked her to tell me what was going on.

"I've got six numbers," she said.

I couldn't think what she was talking about, so I told her to sit down and take a deep breath and to explain to me what she meant. "I've got SIX NUMBERS!" She was yelling it at me. "I've won the jackpot on the National Lottery!"

All I could think was, "Thank the Goddess, my reading had been right." "How can I help you?" I asked.

"I'm so frightened; will you choose a rune for me?"

"Why on earth would you want me to choose a rune if you've just won the Lottery?" I asked.

"For guidance."

I told her to hold on and went to prepare myself and fetch my bag of runes. When I was ready, I went back to the phone. I told her to think about her win and to focus in her mind on what this win would mean to her. When she was ready, I put my hand into my rune-stone pouch and drew out one rune. That rune was Feoh. I later found out that she had won £2.8 million.

Feoh

Feoh, or *Fehu*, represents assets, possessions and wealth. In Native American traditions the buffalo represents abundance. Historically, Feoh represents cattle because anyone who possessed cattle would be considered to be wealthy or financially comfortable.

2

The Story of Ur

THE children played in the sun. Their mothers could hear them laughing as they worked nearby. The atmosphere was one of peace and contentment, but sitting under a tree was one young boy who wasn't as happy as everyone else appeared to be. That morning he had watched the men leaving to go on a hunt to bring back meat for the families of the tribe.

Only the night before, he had asked his father if he could join the hunters. "You are still a boy and not yet ready to hunt," his father told him. "First you must prove yourself to be a man, and then you can join the hunt."

"When can I prove myself a man?" the boy asked his father. "Later my son," he was told.

He sat in the sun watching the other children play. "I am older than them and past childish games," he thought to himself. He knew that his time to prove himself would come, but in his mind, it was not coming soon enough. He wandered aimlessly around the camp; he did not want to join the children. All he wanted was to be able to prove himself a warrior, a hunter, a man. His mother watched discreetly from where she sat with the other women. She felt her son's sadness and wished that she could do something to cheer him, but she knew that he would only be happy when he could prove himself.

She too would be tested. Could she be brave when the day came to let her child go? She had done everything she could to play her part in preparing him for when he would become a man, but she knew in her heart that the day her son left would be the last time she saw her child. When he came back, it would be as a man.

Much later that day, the people of the camp could hear the laughter and rejoicing of the men as they returned victorious from their hunt. The women and children went to meet them and helped to carry their heavy load. The camp became a hive of activity as everyone gathered round to prepare the evening feast and to listen to the tales of courage and bravery.

The boy's father came to sit with him. Sensing his frustration, he told his son how he had felt before he became a man. The boy was comforted to some extent, but this did not completely ease him.

Days passed and still the boy was unsettled, becoming more and more depressed. One day, he saw the elders of the tribe sitting in circle talking. Each time he looked over, he felt that they were talking about him. The next day, the same thing happened and in the days that followed he became more and more convinced that they were indeed discussing him.

And they were. In their wisdom, the elders of the tribe had realised, even before the boy had, that his time to prove himself was approaching. In recent times, his parents would be preparing things for him in readiness for his "change".

"Boy, come here," an elder called to him. The boy was nervous as he made his approach. "It is time to leave childish things behind you now and to prepare for manhood. For the next seven days and nights you will spend time with the elders and you will listen to the secrets that we have to share with you. Go now, tell your family and return to us immediately."

Currents of emotions raced through him. Fear, anticipation, excitement, and dread churned in his stomach. Suddenly, he felt like a child as he ran to his parents.

His mother was filled with anxiety. She wanted her son to be safe and was not ready to see him leave the protection of her hearth, even though she knew that it must be. Now that the time had come, she was fearful, knowing what lay ahead for her son and how easily it could go wrong. And yet she was filled with a sense of pride.

His father too was concerned, but he did not show it as he spoke to his son. "Boy, I hope that I have taught you well and that you have listened to the stories which have been handed down to us from our forefathers. Go now and listen to what you are told. Show your elders respect and value their wisdom. You will leave here our child but when you return, it will be as a man, our son."

The days spent with the elders were long and difficult. Sometimes they fasted, often staying awake long into the night. They practised hunting skills or sat down together to tell him stories, some new and others he had heard many times before.

At midnight on the sixth day, giving him no warning, they woke him and took him outside, before setting off on a mysterious journey. He was tired as he ran alongside them and he wondered where they were going and what would happen. Over hills, across streams and through forests, they travelled until, finally, they arrived at their destination. Through the shadows at the head of a clearing, a huge standing stone could be seen. Surrounding it, smaller stones marked out a circle of power.

They set up a small camp. The cold night air was filled with solemnity as the elders sat in a group and began to take special things from the pouches they carried. He sat and watched with interest, knowing that he had reached the point that he had waited for so long. One elder stepped into the circle of stones and began to light a small fire to prepare a brew. Another elder joined him and began to mix something in a small pot. A third walked round the perimeter of the circle, chanting and singing the praises of those who had gone before. One by one, each of the elders presented him with a gift. One gave him something long and thin wrapped in hide. Another carried in a bundle that was more bulky.

Finally, the last elder took him by the hand and led him into the centre of the circle. The elders stood around the perimeter and raised their arms high above their heads. The boy took their lead and did the same. One of the elders began to hum a single note in a very quiet tone. One by one, the other elders joined him until the chant began to reach a loud crescendo. Suddenly, at the peak of the chant, the rays of the sun broke through the dawn sky and the elders immediately became silent, all quietly revelling in the beauty of the moment. The boy was filled with a sense of wonder as the elders moved towards him, one by one. The first elder blessed him and gave him a warm drink. As he drank, he felt the warmth of the liquid flow down through his body. He knew that this was a very special time. He felt light-headed with hunger and fatigue but at the same time awed by the experience.

The herbs in the drink were beginning to take effect and although he could see, hear and feel everything that was going on, there was an air of detachment within him. He felt as though he was floating on a cloud watching everything from above.

An elder sat before him and began to paint his face and body in a variety of colours, patterns and symbols, to invite the Gods to accompany him and bring him protection and success.

Another of the elders began to beat a drum made of skin and each of the elders began to move and sway or dance to the rhythm. The boy joined them and felt exhilarated by the experience. Round and round they danced and spun until he felt dizzy.

Sometime later, much later, the boy began to wake up. His head felt fuzzy and for a moment he was

unaware of where he was. He began to remember the
chanting, drumming and dancing and, as he looked
around, he could see that he was quite alone. The
stories that the elders had been telling him began to
make sense and he realised that now was the time for
him to prove himself and become a man. His survival
depended on himself – not his mother or father or the
warriors or hunters. Fear gripped the pit of his
stomach. He had no choice now but to survive by his
wits and his newfound knowledge.

The boy began to open one of the hide parcels that
he had been given and to his amazement and delight
he discovered that the first contained a beautiful
hunting spear. Unlike the play spear that he and the
other boys were familiar with, this was the spear of a
hunter. The shaft was strong and long and carved with
magickal symbols. He caressed the spear lovingly as he
turned it in his hands, enjoying the feel of the smooth-
ness and balance. His eyes were filled with wonder as
he looked at it.

Another hide bundle contained several items. The
first things that he noticed were a water carrier and a
sling. He realised instantly that these were the same
ones he had watched his father make. The next thing
to catch his eye was a hide pouch that he had watched

his mother sew. Inside the pouch were some perfectly smooth stones that he could use with the sling. His pouch held herbs for sustenance and healing, wrapped in smaller parcels. Among his other gifts were a hunting dagger and an axe.

He could use the hides for warmth and to make a shelter in the night. He wrapped one of these around his shoulders and gathered up his belongings. He slipped the pouch over his head and under his arm, letting its strap rest across his chest. He then tied the axe and dagger to the belt around his waist and carried the spear in his hand as he set off to explore his surroundings. The day was long as he walked and hunger gnawed at his belly. He came across a stream, took a long, cool drink and filled his water bottle. He realised that he would have to find food soon, so he began to move more silently through the brush.

A rabbit was his first kill, but that was easy. Children could hunt and catch rabbits and he knew that if he were to prove himself, it would take more than a rabbit to do so. As night began to fall, he looked for somewhere to set up camp so that he could skin and cook his rabbit and get some sleep. The stars were bright and the moon was full as he settled down under his shelter made from dried branches, covered with hide.

Early the next morning, he awoke and began again to explore and hunt. The days passed slowly. Finding game to hunt was more difficult than he had thought. Suddenly, he heard movement; crouching low he waited and watched. A huge male aurochs was grazing nearby. This was far too big a test for him. He could never kill such a large beast. And yet, was this not what he had been waiting for, the chance to prove that he was a great hunter, a strong man? He sat quietly and watched the aurochs' movements. For three days he did nothing but follow and watch the great beast. How could he kill it? Hunger gnawed at him and he had to break his watch to hunt small prey or catch fish to feed himself. He lay in his shelter that night thinking of how he could kill the aurochs and, even if he could kill it, how could he carry it back to his tribe? He began to make a plan. He had noticed that the aurochs had grazed near a large rocky outcrop. If he climbed to the top of the highest rock and the aurochs passed under it, he could jump down onto its back and spear it.

On the fourth day, he rose early and began to prepare himself. He painted his face and body with the symbols that he had seen the elders use. He tested his spear, feeling the weight and balance in his hand.

When he had done all he could, he set off to find the aurochs. He reached the outcrop of rocks and climbed to the top, but there was no sign of the beast. All day he waited, but the aurochs didn't come. As night began to fall, he wondered if it would ever come back. He began to regret his idea and he felt cold and hungry. And yet something made him stay. He lay down on the rocks and drifted in and out of sleep. Before he knew it, dawn was breaking.

Suddenly, he heard a familiar snort and he realised that the aurochs was below him. He grabbed his dagger and before he even realised what he was doing, he was leaping from the rock onto the aurochs' back. He landed square on the beast and the animal went berserk. It was bucking and rearing and charging about, trying to shake off whatever was on its back. The boy was struggling to keep his hold and trying to avoid being gored by its huge horns. He plunged the dagger into the aurochs' neck over and over again, but the beast became more enraged. The boy thought he was going to be killed. Blood was spraying everywhere. Again and again the aurochs bucked and suddenly the boy was flying through the air. He felt a horn rip his side as he was thrown and blackness descended on him as he hit the ground.

Pain, excruciating pain, was all he could feel as he drifted back into consciousness. All was quiet around him. For a moment he did not know where he was. Then panic hit as he remembered what he had done. As best he could, he picked himself up and to his amazement the aurochs lay some distance away. Tentatively, he made his way towards the giant beast. A huge pool of blood surrounded the wounds on the animal's neck. He knelt on the ground and cried.

He was ashamed that he had been the one to take the aurochs' life but, at the same time, he felt proud that he had achieved this great kill. He smeared the blood of his kill over his face and chest, stood up and raised his hands above his head and gave thanks to the Gods who had protected him and helped him win his mighty battle. Much work was yet to be done because now he would have to find some way to clean and prepare the meat for the journey back to the tribe. But first he must attend to his wounds. He climbed the outcrop to gather his things and, as he made his way back down, he collected pieces of dried wood to make a fire.

Back at his camp, he warmed some water on the fire and added the herbs his mother had prepared for him. After he had dressed his wounds, he stretched a hide between two pieces of wood to allow him to drag some of the meat and the precious horns back to his village. What he couldn't take back, he wrapped in a skin and buried under some rocks.

As he approached the village, he could hear the children shouting and announcing his arrival. His parents, the elders and everyone from the tribe gathered to watch him and, as he drew closer, they ran to join him. Suddenly, he was hoisted shoulder-high and his burden was taken from him. Finally with his feet back on the ground, one of the elders called: "Who is this man come among us bearing the meat and horns from the giant aurochs?" His father stepped forward to claim him. "This man is my son," he announced proudly.

Ur

Ur or *Uruz* represents challenge. It is symbolised by an auroch or ox. Known as the rune of passage, Ur represents death of the old and birth of the new.

3

The Story of Thorn

SHE was lying back in her bath enjoying the luxury of some quiet time to herself. The children were away on a school trip, her husband was at work and she had nothing pressing to do and no one to please but herself. She had spent time preparing her bath: placing several small candles at each corner and adding some patchouli essential oil while the water was running. She loved the smell of patchouli. She had left the bathroom door open so that she could listen to her favourite calming music.

As she lay there listening and soaking up the ambience of the atmosphere that she had carefully created, she thought of the evening ahead. After her bath, she would book a table for dinner at the local hotel for herself and her husband. She was pleased with herself and with her plan. Her husband had been working really hard over the past few months. The company he was employed by had been taken over recently and there had been a few redundancies but, thankfully, he had been kept on. He loved his job and couldn't imagine doing anything else, but the recent changes had meant that he had to work longer hours than usual. She felt as though they had hardly seen each other. This special time tonight would be really good for them.

The phone ringing interrupted her daydream. She would just let it ring, the answer-phone would record a message and she would deal with whatever or whoever it was later. She heard the machine click on and her greeting being played to the caller. Then she heard her husband's voice: "Are you there? Pick up, sweetheart, it's important." She quickly jumped out of the bath, grabbed her towelling bathrobe and was pulling it on as she hurried to the phone.

"Thank God that you are there," said her husband, relieved. "Sorry to spring this on you at short notice, babe, but you will never believe what I have to tell you. I have been offered a directorship in the company with the new owner. He is only here for a couple of days, so I have invited him and his wife home for dinner. We will be there in about an hour."

After a brief chat, pretending that everything was fine, she began to hastily prepare for the evening ahead. She wrapped her wet hair in a towel and threw on a pair of tracksuit trousers and a T-shirt. For the next half-hour she raced about. "Some prawns defrosted would make a nice starter in a prawn cocktail," she thought, "and there were enough bits and pieces in the fridge that she could pull together a stir-fry and serve it up with rice." Just before they were due to arrive, she looked over the lounge to make sure that everything was in order. "Flowers, that's what was missing," she told herself.

There were some large white marguerites growing in the garden and some beautifully scented roses. She could pick the marguerites without any difficulty, but she would have to find her secateurs and gloves to pick the roses. She knew that the marguerites would be lovely in a display and that the roses would add a delightful fragrance to the room. She had just finished arranging the flowers and managed to throw something "respectable" on, when her husband and their guests arrived. The evening was a success, everyone enjoyed each other's company and the meal was delicious. Before leaving, the woman said to her: "Your roses are lovely; my husband and I grow roses at home and I know how difficult it is to pick them without ripping your hands to bits. I really appreciate the effort that you have made and at such short notice too. It was

Thorn

Thorn or *Thurizas* advises us to exercise caution, to handle things with care. It accompanies situations where it is prudent to give due consideration to circumstances before acting.

41

4

The Story of Ansur

'I don't know what I am going to do," she said to her friend. "I love him so much and I am sure that he loves me, but we just keep fighting with each other. It's like we can't talk any more. Take yesterday for instance, my stomach was churning the whole day thinking about the argument that we had had the night before. We both got up in the morning, got ready for work and left the house with hardly a word to each other. I made up my mind that when I got home, I would cook a nice meal and open a bottle of wine, like we used to do when we were first married. But when I got home, there was a message on the answer phone from him saying that he wouldn't be in until late. I was so angry that I just thought, 'Damn him, he can be like that if he wants to, I don't care.' He could have called me on my mobile but, plainly, he didn't want to talk to me, so left a message on the house phone instead."

She sat on her best friend's sofa with her head resting in her hands. The tears fell, but there was no relief. She just felt that everything that she had believed in was falling apart and she didn't know what to do.

"How long has it been like this?" her friend asked.

"It's been six months now and I don't know how it began. I just know that we seem to be in a rut of snapping at each other. We used to be so close and shared such special times together. My heart is breaking and I can't bear the thought of us splitting up. He looks so unhappy too. He used to hum to himself and was always so eager to please me and now it's as though he just wants to fight with me all the time."

"What kind of things does he say that upsets you?"

"It's not so much what he says but the way that he says things, and then it all starts again and we end up not speaking at all."

While they chatted, her friend brought out a small velvet pouch and handed it to her.

"What's this?" she asked, examining the contents.

"They're my rune stones. I always find them helpful if I am anxious or confused about something."

"What should I do with them?"

"Nothing yet, just hold them. Put your hand inside the bag and just feel them. You will be drawn to one as we speak, and it may help you."

Doing as she was told, she put her hand into the pouch and allowed the stones to fall through her fingers again and again, as they spoke. After a while, she realised that she was holding onto one particular stone. It almost felt as though it was burning, such was the heat from it.

"I think I have found the one that I want," she told her friend.

"Go on then, take it out and let me see it."

She slowly took the stone out of the pouch and turned it over to look at it.

"It looks like the letter *f*. Do you know what that means?" she asked her friend.

"Yes, I do. It is called Ansur and it is the rune of communication."

"But that's the problem," she wailed, "we can't communicate, we just argue. It's a solution I am looking for."

"This is your solution. Stop arguing and start communicating."

"I have been trying to do that for six months."

"Well clearly you are not going about it the right way, so this is what I suggest. Call him now and ask him what time he will be home. Tell him that you are preparing his favourite meal and that you want to talk to him about something important."

"But what if he says that he won't be home till late?"

"Tell him that you will wait up and have a late supper with him."

"What will I do if an argument starts?"

"As soon as you feel that one is starting, take a deep breath and remember how much you love each other. Go to him and hold his hands and look into his eyes. Tell him that you love him and tell him how it makes you feel when he says certain things to you. Tell him that you know that some of the things you say to him hurt his feelings too and that you want all that to stop now. Try it. Go on, wash your face and get yourself home, you have a lot to organise. Call me tomorrow and let me know how you are."

The next day she called her friend.

"Hi, it's me. I don't know how to thank you," she said. "We were awake the whole night talking, and there was so much that we had both misunderstood. We both felt as though we were communicating again."

"Good I'm glad that it worked out for you two."

"We are going to go away for a romantic weekend, but I was wondering, could you tell me where I can get some runes?"

Ansur

Ansur or *Ansuz* is the rune of communication and advises us to listen as well as speak. Communication in some form or another will be important.

5

The Story of Rad

HE HAD always been a bit of a loner, but over the last year he had begun to realise that he was missing the friendship of others in his life. But it's always the same when you build walls around yourself, eventually they become so high that even you find it difficult to get over or penetrate them. Making new friends was not easy; most people were already established in their circle of friends and he was so out of practice at socialising that he wasn't even sure people would find him interesting enough to want to spend time with him. He didn't play football or even watch it on television. His taste in music leaned more towards the 60s than the present day. The problem was that he was quite set in his ways and found it difficult to change his outlook. That was until about three months ago when he met Rado.

Now and again, Rado would give him a call and invite him to come over to his house. It was easier that way because Rado didn't drive and they lived quite a distance from each other. He had a car, so it was no bother really. Usually during these visits, Rado would suggest an outing. Recently, more than once, he had wondered to himself why Rado was friendly with him. They did not seem to have anything in common at all, but he had been glad of the company anyway. He had looked forward to going out with him – or he did until recently.

Over the past couple of weeks he had begun to realise that Rado had many other friends and often went out with them without inviting him along. He had wondered why, but it was only now that the true picture was beginning to emerge. Rado only invited him when he wasn't able to get a lift from any of his other friends. In short, he was being used because he had transport. At first when he realised this, he was annoyed. He felt as though he was being duped and that it was a false friendship. But then he began to look at it from another angle. He too was using Rado. He was using him for company. He made up his mind. Rado could have as many hidden agendas as he wanted, as long as he knew and understood that, then there would be no problem.

Rad

Rad or *Rado* represents the turning of the wheel. In today's society, this can represent transport and matters connected to it. It may be you who is making a journey or someone may be making a journey towards you. The reason for this may not be as apparent as you would think and as long as you understand this, you will come to no harm. If you are gullible, however, you may be taken in by false hopes.

6

The Story of Ken

THE people lived within sight of the angry
mountain. Occasionally, they could hear it
rumbling and growling and they would look
to each other and pause. Some had travelled to the
mountain's edge to beg the mountain God to be kind
to them. Some had even ventured further up and came
back with tales of strange rock formations and of pools
of water, which spat and foamed.

In their language, the name for the angry mountain
God was Volkano. Their shamans told them of a time
when the angry mountain became so furious that it lit
up the night sky with a glowing red fire and spat out
its anger with such force that it spilled over onto the
land and flowed down to the valleys below, killing
everything in its path.

The stories told of how, long ago, one brave man
stole light from fire that fell from the sky, to make a
torch for his people.

That light still burned and all the people of the

camp took turns to keep it alive. They called it Kano. It brought welcome warmth. For them Kano was a symbol of light and where there was light, there was action or the ability or opportunity for action. They could do things with light and fire that they could not have done otherwise. The cooked with it, they warmed themselves and they gathered together around it after dark to talk and tell their stories.

It's destructive power was respected, revered and even welcomed, for as the forest fire destroys the life in its path, so does that destruction leave the way clear for brave new shoots to grow.

Fire from Kano brought action, renewal and it brought opportunity.

Ken

Ken or *Kano* symbolises an opening, an offer or a new beginning. It foretells of action in some situation that perhaps has been stagnant, or movement in your life where previously there was stillness.

7

The Story of Geofu

MOTHER and Father sat side by side. They both knew what the other was thinking, but neither of them wanted to put their thoughts into words. Finally, Father did: "We don't know all that much about him."

"We know that they seem to be happy together," answered Mother.

"It's one thing being happy, but marriage?"

"Well, they have been seeing each other for nearly a year now. We were together only a few months when we decided that we were going to marry."

"Yes, but you could trust me, and I could trust you to keep the promises that we made to each other."

"Anyway," mother said, "they'll be here soon."

Just at that moment, the young couple arrived. Their daughter looked extremely happy as she led the way into the lounge.

"Look, Mum, Dad," she said, as she held out her left hand to proudly show them her engagement ring.

It was beautiful. In the middle of the gold ring sat an X-shape with a diamond set in the centre of the cross. "Oh," said Mother. "That looks as though the diamond is set in a kiss."

"Actually, Mum, it's an ancient symbol that we thought would seal our love, it is called Geofu and it means promise. We have made promises to each other that we intend to keep," said her daughter.

Mother and Father looked at each other, a knowing look, and then they smiled and hugged them both.

Father opened a bottle of malt whisky that he had been keeping for a special occasion and poured a glass for him and his son-in-law to be. He felt more confident now that they would be good for each other and would have a strong future ahead of them.

Geofu

The symbol Geofu or *Gefu* is the most widely used symbol in today's society. How many times have you ended a letter or a card to someone you care for with an X to represent a kiss? Geofu stands for promises made.

8

The Story of Wynn

S HE sat by the fire enjoying the warmth from the burning logs, wondering how her husband was getting on with his interview. He had been studying for such a long time and had often felt that he just wanted to give up. They were just an ordinary couple; both had left school around the same time without any formal qualifications. They both found jobs in a nearby factory, he on the factory floor and she in the office as an office junior. That's where they met and fell in love.

They had been married for a year when he decided that he wanted to do something more with his life. He had approached the personnel department and asked if there were any training courses available. After a series of interviews with the management, they agreed to put him through training. They were happy with his attendance record at work and in the way that he dealt with any problems that arose, but he would have to work very hard to maintain his income and attend college on day release. He would also have to study most evenings and this would mean a change in their lifestyle. No more socialising – they wouldn't be able to afford it; if he was studying, he couldn't work over-time, as he had done in the past. She was prepared to make any sacrifice to help him, but for the past three years it had become harder and harder. Sometimes he would be depressed and she would have to encourage him; other times when he was up, she would be down in the dumps.

The exams were over now and the results had been sent to his employers. He was meeting with his bosses now. She wondered what the outcome would be, especially now that she was pregnant. It had been a long, hard struggle, but if he passed, and was given the promotion that he so desperately wanted, then everything would be fine. But if he hadn't …

The time seemed to drag on endlessly, she got up and made another cup of coffee and went back to sit in front of the fire. She was worried, he would be so disappointed and so would she if he had failed. What would they do then, she wondered? She kept looking at her watch, but that didn't make time go any faster. She closed her eyes and before she knew it, she had drifted off to sleep. As she slept, she dreamt. Her husband was running towards her laughing and waving his arms in the air. He was carrying tools in one hand and in the other a scroll of paper. He was saying something to her, but she could not quite make out what it was. Her heart was racing with excitement and an eager smile was on her face. It slowly began to dawn on her what he was saying: "Wake up."

She jumped and then relaxed as she realised that he was home and, what's more, he was grinning from ear to ear. He knelt beside her and took her in his arms. He held her close to him.

"Everything is going to be fantastic," he told her.

He had passed his exams and his employers were so impressed with his results that they not only promoted him, they gave him his own department and a company car. They were both filled with joy, the kind of joy that Wynn heralds.

Wynn

One of the best Runic symbols to have in a forecast, Wynn or *Wunjo* is connected with great happiness and success. Sometimes it can indicate travel associated with this success.

9

The Story of Hagall

THE two young women had prepared themselves for the walk that they were undertaking and had been looking forward to it too. They were using part of their annual holiday to help raise money for charity

During the first part of their vacation they would walk the West Highland Way, starting just outside Glasgow – 95 miles in all – and some people had sponsored them as much as £5 for every mile. They were excited at the prospect of the adventure that lay ahead and a little apprehensive too. They both enjoyed walking but had never attempted anything as long as this. They were glad that the second part of their holiday would be spent relaxing in a nice guesthouse in Fort William. Many of their friends and sponsors had come to see them off and there was a buzz of excitement in the air.

A final check of their rucksacks and it was time to begin. They were happy and smiling as everyone cheered and waved them off. It wasn't too long before they settled down into a steady routine and during their walk they chatted about life and different experiences that they had had. At the end of each day, they found somewhere to set up their tent and prepare an evening meal.

On the last day, they decided to make an early start. The weather so far had been good to them, but the sky looked heavy and overcast and they did not want to be caught in a storm in the middle of nowhere. The gentle breeze had become a wind, and their faces were being stung by the strength of it. Just as they reached the top of a hill, the wind suddenly died down and there was stillness all around them. They stopped too to admire what little they could see and to wonder at the peacefulness. Suddenly, without any warning, the skies opened and hailstones rained down on them. There was nowhere to shelter. All they could do was to pull their tent out and hold it over them till the storm abated. The ground was white with a thick covering of hailstones. Then, just as suddenly as the hailstorm had begun, it ended.

They crept out from under their shelter as the skies cleared above them. The sun broke through and shone on them and there, below them, stretched Fort

William. A rainbow arched above the town. It was the most beautiful thing that they had seen on their journey. They looked at each other and laughed. They stuffed the sodden tent back into the rucksack and hurried down the hill, looking forward to the reception committee that would be waiting for them and to a long, hot, luxurious bath. The ferocity of the sudden storm had delayed them, but it had not prevented them from reaching their goal.

Hagall

Hagall predicts the unexpected. Generally, foreseeing a problem that must be overcome before you can move forward.

10

The Story of Nied

'DO YOU ever feel as though you are taking three steps forward and two back? I feel as though the past few months have been an endless struggle and everything that I try to do is prevented by outside forces." The young girl sat on the end of her friend's bed with her head in her hands, a look of despair etched on her face.

"Hmm ..." came the slow reply.

"Are you listening or are you just pretending to? Here I am, looking for guidance and my best mate can only grunt."

"No! I am listening but I am thinking too."

"Well if you are, you will be the only one. I don't feel as if anyone is listening."

"Have you ever heard of the Cabbala?"

"Yeah, it's something to do with magick isn't it? Anyway, what does that have to do with what I'm talking about?"

"Cabbalists use numbers and geometry and believe

that the universe is a grand plan, not just a haphazard sequence of events."

"And?"

"The Cabbala is like a tree, the roots, deep in the ground, and the trunk pushing its way up to the sky. The branches spread themselves wide and high. Each branch has smaller branches and they too have even smaller ones sprouting from them. Each spring, new life surges through the tree and even more new branches begin to grow."

"Well I can see how you might have thought that that small piece of useless information might help me. Thanks."

"Useless information! Pay attention to what I am saying, and you might find the answer to your dilemma."

"I'm sorry. I shouldn't be sarcastic. I am really feeling sorry for myself. So tell me about the tree."

"Don't think too much about the tree, but think about the branches. Imagine the tree spreading its branches further and further, and higher and higher. What do you think the tree is doing?"

"It's reaching out."

"Yes, but for what?"

"Light."

"Precisely."

"Well?"

"Light is life, it's knowledge, it's the answer."

"You are not helping at all."

"Think of yourself as the tree, imagine that your feet are the roots, your body the trunk, and your head and arms the branches. Picture yourself reaching out. Tell me in one word what you are searching for?"

"Success."

"Think now of the branches of the tree, each and every one of these branches is a path; each path has a name, just like street names on a road map. Some paths lead to nowhere. Some lead to an obstruction, which, even if you overcome that obstacle, you would only encounter another, like knots in a piece of wood. Other paths lead to success."

"Ah, now I am beginning to see what you are talking about."

"Each path that you have chosen has been blocked. It is time to choose another path, another destination."

"You're right, you know I feel really lightened."

"That's because you have just been enlightened."

"What was the name of the branch that has the knots in it, you know the one that obstructs you?"

"Nied."

Nied

Nied or *Nauthiz* or *Naudhiz* is a barrier or an obstacle that stops or prevents you from doing something, going somewhere or achieving something.

11

The Story of Is

'I AM just going to tell them exactly what I think of them, they have pushed me too far this time," she said to her friend. "I have done more than my fair share and the more I do, the more they seem to expect of me; enough is enough. I've had it. I am going to call them and tell them what I think, and then I am going to resign and look for another job."

"I think that you should wait, you are angry just now. Act in haste and rue the day, so the saying goes."

"Can you blame me for being so angry? They just seem to want more and more and it's always me they expect to step into the breach when someone is off on holiday or off sick and, like a fool, I always end up doing it."

"So what's tipped you over the edge this time?"

"They have asked me to go in on my one day off this week, and I had planned to do absolutely nothing for a change. I am always running about and never get time to myself. I wanted to have a long-lie and get up when I felt like it, maybe take a long bath and then treat myself to lunch and some shopping, just anything really that didn't involve work."

"I thought that you loved your work."

"I do, but I feel as though they are taking advantage of me."

"Maybe they are testing you."

"How do you mean?"

"Maybe they have plans for you that they haven't told you about, and all this extra work is a way of seeing if you can cope."

"They could have told me."

"But if they had told you then your actions would be calculated rather than spontaneous."

"What if they are not testing me and are just taking advantage of me?"

"Why don't you draw a rune for advice on how you should act or react to this current situation?"

"OK. What do we do?"

Her friend got up and went to fetch an ornate wooden box from the bookshelf then sat down beside her. Placing both hands on the box, she sat quietly for some moments and then said: "I want you to put both hands on the box, just as I did, then think about your intention to tell your employers how angry you feel and that you want to resign. When you feel as though you have gone over this clearly in your mind, I want you to put your hand into the box and draw out one rune stone and let me see it."

She did as she was asked and when she was ready, she put her hand into the box. She knew that all the stones were the same shape, but she felt as though one of them was a little different from the others. She held on to that one, withdrew her hand from the box and gave the rune to her friend.

"Which one did I choose?" she asked.

Her friend turned the stone round and let her see it.

"It's just a straight line! What is it and what does it mean?"

"Its called Is or Isa and it means that you are treading on thin ice."

"I don't understand?"

"It means that you should delay making any decisions or changes at this time. Basically, it is telling you to wait."

She sighed with frustration.

"How long should I wait?"

"Until something changes."

"How long do you think that will be?"

"I always feel that the change will be soon, otherwise a different rune would have been chosen. Just be patient. Go in on your day off, as they have asked you to, and take it from there."

A week later, she called round to see her friend again.

"How are things at work then?" her friend asked.

"That's why I came to see you today," she said, as she hugged her.

"What's the hug for?" her friend asked, smiling.

"For being right and for stopping me from doing something that I would have regretted for a long time."

"What's happened?"

"Well, when I went in on my day off, I was called into the boss's office. He thanked me for all the effort that I had made and now I've been given a huge bonus and offered a promotion. I am so excited, and I just can't thank you enough. I might have lost the chance if it hadn't been for your good advice."

"It wasn't my advice, it was the rune's advice."

I_s

Is or *Isa* extends a warning to allow things to remain as they are for the time being. Like the old saying, "You are treading on thin ice", Is implies that to go further or to take action at this time will create difficulties for you.

12
The Story of Jara

SHE took a great deal of pleasure from her garden. As she sat there basking in the heat of the warm summer sun, the flowerbeds awash with colour, she was proud of her efforts. Blooms flourished all around her and new buds promised even yet more colour to come. Her friends would be here soon to share a light lunch and she knew that they too would enjoy the tranquillity and peace that her garden offered. A small stream trickled close by, the comforting sound of it mingled with the tinkle of the garden chimes she had hung from the branches of the trees. A bright windsock swayed gently and the birds chirped merrily around the feeders that she kept well stock with wild bird food. One by one her friends arrived, each complimenting her, as she knew they would. She went inside to fetch the sandwiches and cakes that she had prepared and on her return, she could hear her friends chatting about her.

"I don't know how she does it; this garden is

spectacular. It must be magick," said one friend as she approached with a laden tray.

"No it's not magick," she replied as she put the tray on the table, "It's effort. I love my garden and I spend any spare time I have in it."

"I spend a lot of time in my garden too, but it never grows like yours does. There must be more to it. So tell us what your secret is?" another friend enquired.

"No secret really, I treat my garden as I treat my friends and the people I love or care for. I remember once reading somewhere, 'Friendship is like a garden. In order for it to bloom and flourish it has to be nurtured and cared for'. I try to do both."

"Well you make great sandwiches."

They all laughed together.

Still curious, one of her friends asked: "So tell us, how do you nurture your garden?"

"Well, what do you do with yours? Where do you get your plants and what do you do with them?"

"I get mine from the garden centre or sometimes the supermarket."

"Then what do you do?"

"I stick them in the ground and hope that they will grow. Where do you get yours?"

"Same place."

"Well, what do you do that's so different and that rewards you with such beauty?"

"No matter where I get my plants, I give them a long soak first and while they are soaking I prepare the area where I am going to plant them. I dig the hole, put in some plant food and water it well before putting in the plant. While I am doing that, I mentally introduce it to all my other plants. Each day, when I come into the garden, I mentally thank them and I make sure that they are growing well. A little effort goes a long way. Have you ever heard of the rune stone Jara?"

"I've heard of rune stones. What's particular about that one?"

"Jara is the rune of harvest and its basic translation means you will reap what you have sown."

Jara

Jara or *Gera* helps one to understand that efforts made will be justly rewarded. The more effort put in, the greater the reward. Less effort will result in less of a reward.

13
The Story of Yr

'NEW Year's Eve and here I am struggling through three feet of snow in the cold and dark trying to find a fault in the electricity supply. I hate this job. One day I am going to pack it in," he thought to himself. His feet were cold, in spite of the thick socks and the heavy boots. His colleague trudged along behind him, too wrapped up in his own misery to care.

He went on mumbling to himself: "People are so ungrateful; you would think it was our fault that there was a power failure. They are greedy, that's what they are, greedy, heartless and inconsiderate of anyone but themselves. They leave lights on all over the place just because they can afford to. If they had any idea how these things worked, they would maybe think about turning out lights that aren't needed. It would soon mount up and then I wouldn't be called out on Hogmanay to mend damage caused by excessive demands on the system."

The men knew that the fault was within a specific area, but the snow was falling so hard that they could only see a few feet ahead. He felt as though they had been walking for ages.

"Shouldn't be too far now," he said turning to where his colleague should have been. But there was no sign of him. "Where the devil is he?" he thought.

"Eddie," he called. "Eddie where are you?" He tried to get his bearings, but the blizzard was blowing so hard that he wasn't even sure of which direction he had been travelling. Everything around him was a blur. He could feel panic setting in and had to struggle to keep calm. He peered back in the direction that he thought he had come from. There was no hope of seeing a light, thanks to this massive power failure but, with any luck, he might see the torchlight of some of the other electricians. He knew that they wouldn't be too far away. He tried using his mobile phone, but the signal was weak and he couldn't make a connection.

"Eddie!" he called. "Eddieee!" yelling now.

He had been trudging through the snow for about 10 minutes, calling his workmate's name. He was afraid that he might have been going round in circles and would not be able to find him.

But suddenly a voice rang out: "Over here. I'm over

here. Help me! I'm over here," his colleague yelled.

"Thank you, God," he said aloud, then followed the direction of the voice. He practically fell over his friend, who was huddled in a heap on the ground.

"You will have to get help. I think I have broken my leg," his injured colleague moaned.

What happened to you? One minute you were there and the next you were gone."

"I fell down a hole; couldn't see it for the snow."

"You hang in there, Eddie, I think I can find my way back. If I keep going downhill, I should meet the road where we parked the van."

"Don't be too long mate. I'm in agony here and be careful, please."

Although it felt like an age, it really wasn't too long before he came across the fence surrounding the field that they had been crossing. He knew that if he followed the fence he would reach the van, but he was afraid that he wouldn't be able to retrace his steps and find his colleague again. He took off his scarf and tied it round the fence to give him a marker, so that he could lead the ambulance men to his injured colleague, then set off. It was with a sense of great relief that he saw the van looming out of the blizzard ahead of him. He clambered in, pulled out his phone and was amazed to see that the signal was strong and he was able to phone for help.

When the emergency services arrived, he managed to lead them back to the marker he had attached to the fence. Finding his friend wasn't so easy, but they eventually got to him and were able to carry him safely back to the ambulance on a stretcher. Another repair team were sent out to find and fix the power failure and, after a quick check up at the hospital, he was allowed home in time to celebrate the New Year with his family, some of whom had flown in from New Zealand for a once-in-a-lifetime visit.

The next day, the newspapers were full of the story. The headline was, "Repair man's heroic New Year rescue bid". He was being hailed as a hero but all he could think of was that it could all have ended so differently.

Yr

Yr or *Eiwaz* teaches us that the going may be difficult and there may be unforeseen obstacles but eventually with persistence you will reach your destination.

14
The Story of Peorth

TO begin with, she booked an appointment for a tarot and rune reading roughly twice a year. She had a busy life. As well as looking after her family and running a home, she also ran two businesses. She found the readings helpful and had come to depend on the guidance offered, particularly when making business decisions. More often than not, she requested a six-month rune forecast. Her reader would tell her to think of the events that she knew would be happening during the next six months and to ask for guidance on them. But the readings also gave pointers to events she had no way of knowing would occur. While she was astounded by the accuracy of the tarot readings, it was the rune forecasts that really amazed her.

Recently, the period between consultations was becoming shorter and shorter. Even her reader was becoming concerned at the increased frequency of her visits, fearing that she was becoming too dependent on them. The woman had thought deeply about this and had come to the conclusion that she was going to have to broach this, even though it might mean losing a regular client. She was due for a reading that day. The reader decided that when her client arrived, she would tell her that she had to be responsible for making her own choices and decisions in life and in business. She would tell her that this would be the last reading that she would give her for at least six months.

When the client arrived, the reader made her some coffee and they both sat down to begin the reading. They began with the tarot cards and the reading was mainly similar to her last one, which came as no surprise to either reader or client. But they both knew that it was the rune reading that she was waiting for.

The reader began preparing her rune cards, spreading them in a circle as she always did. "Think of one question and choose your answer," the reader said. The woman did as she was told and pointed to the card of her choice.

It was Peorth. "This is the rune of mystery and hidden information. It could indicate that, in due course, information pertaining to your question will be revealed to you but not at this time," the reader said, before she gathered the cards, shuffled them and spread them in a circle again. She told the woman to think of her next question and again to choose the card that held the answer. She took her time scanning the cards and finally made her choice by pointing to the card she wanted. Again the reader turned the card over and it was Peorth. "Did you think of the same question?" the reader asked.

"No. It was a different question."

"Perhaps it links in some unknown way to the first question."

For the third time, the reader gathered the cards and prepared them in the usual way and told the woman to think of her third question and choose the card that contained the answer. She pointed to the card of her choice and the reader turned it over. It was Peorth! The reader gathered the cards together and told the women that the time had come for her to make her own choices. She told her that she was becoming too dependent on having readings. "But I asked a different question!" she exclaimed.

"Yes, but you are asking far too many. It will be at least six months before I read for you again."

There are occasions, or situations in our life, where guidance can be sought and given using the ancient oracles, but this client had become too dependent and was becoming unable to make even everyday choices without consulting the oracle.

Peorth

Peorth or *Perth* or *Perthro* is the rune of mystery and hidden information and it tells us that we must wait for information to be revealed to us at the right and proper time.

15
The Story of Eolh

THE small child ran about the toy superstore, excited by all the bright colours and mountains of toys. The store was full and nobody paid particular attention. Most people were there with their own children and their thoughts were taken up with what they were looking for and the cost of the items on display. The child's mother was nearby and, to all intents and purposes, it looked as though she was not paying attention to her child at all. The store was full of people, mostly parents with children, but there were a few adults on their own, obviously browsing for birthday gifts or special treats for loved ones.

One man looked a little out of place. It would be hard to put your finger on why, exactly, but his behaviour did seem a little odd. The mother glanced up every now and again, to see what her daughter was up to and had to call to her two or three times to keep the little girl in her sight. Mostly, however, it looked as though she wasn't paying any attention at all. The little girl was the youngest of three children and her mum had a lot on her mind. As well as trying to shop for her eldest child's birthday, she was a little preoccupied with, firstly, finding what she was looking for; secondly, if she would be able to afford it; thirdly, how she was going to hide it until the following day. There was also the weekly shop to think about before getting home in time for school coming out and two hungry children arriving home.

The little girl had no such cares. A pretty little thing with blonde hair and bright blue, innocent eyes, all she could think about was dolls, soft toys, prams and bikes, and things to climb in and out of.

Finally, her mum found what she was looking for. She checked her purse to make sure that she had enough cash to pay for it and still get all the other things that she needed for her shopping. She called to her daughter and together the two of them made their way to the till. The gift was so big that she needed both hands to carry it to the check out. She wished that she had taken a trolley, but she was nearly there now and her little girl was trotting happily behind her. They waited in the queue together. Suddenly the mother realised that her daughter had gone very quiet. She looked down to where she should have been, but she was gone.

In a moment that felt like an eternity, the distraught mother scanned the shop floor and quickly spied the child being led out of the store by the man who had looked out of place. In that one second, she took in the whole picture. She dropped everything – her handbag, the shopping, the toy – and ran at them. She didn't utter a sound, but anger and panic surged through her. She slapped the man on the shoulder and, as he turned round, she balled her fist and punched him hard in the stomach with all her strength. Two security guards appeared as if by magick, for they had seen the whole thing on the store's security cameras. They grappled the man to the floor as she dropped to her knees and hugged her child close to her. "Look mummy the nice man gave me a doll," said the little girl. The mother made sure that the child could not see the man being hustled away to await the arrival of the police. The staff were very kind and took both of them to the customer services room and made her a cup of tea. They telephoned her husband at his work so that he could come and fetch them.

"I knew there was something strange about him," she told her husband that night. "I almost felt as though he was following us about, but I thought I was just being silly. I can't believe how close we came to losing her."

The woman may have looked as though she wasn't watching her little girl, but she was. And when it was needed, she was there to protect her.

Eolh

Eolh or *Elhaz* or *Algiz* is the rune of protection and has strong connections to the mother figure. It shows us when it is safe for us to undertake any task.

16
The Story of Sigel

SOME time ago, I heard of a story about a connection between the ancient runes and Germany and Great Britain during the Second World War. The story, as I remember it, was that Hitler and his associates had formed a coven, or a following, for the sole purpose of working black magick to empower themselves when fighting against Britain. The story goes that they took some ancient runes and bound them together creating a "bind" rune. They took two images of the rune Yr and laid them across each other to form a circle. The end of one symbol touched the beginning of the other. As mentioned earlier, Yr teaches us that the going may be difficult and there may be unforeseen obstacles, but eventually, with persistence, you will reach your destination. Over these two symbols they laid two images of Sigel side by side. Sigel is the rune that symbolises victory.

In magick, I believe that the first step is to think of your desire, using your crown chakra. The next step is to see your desire by visualising it in your third eye chakra. Next, you speak of your desire using your throat chakra, you embrace your desire using your heart chakra, you empower your desire by using your solar plexus chakra, and so on and so forth. During that process we can go on furthering our desire by writing our desire, carving images, gathering friends around us to join in our attempts. If you have read my *Book Of Spells* you will know the rules: whatever you do will come back to you, and, never interfere with or try to change another person's will using magick.

Hitler and his following had tried to do all of this to win their war using black magick. They had meetings that opened and closed with the words Sieg heil. The same words were used as a salute and around this were formed a group known, and feared by many, as the SS. Ultimately, Hitler lost the war and took his own life. I believe, because he tried to use Sacred Ancient Wisdom with evil intent, he and many of his followers suffered for breaking the rules: "If it harms none, do as you will. Whatever you do will come back to you threefold." This led to the downfall of Hitler. But Sigel is not about defeat; it is about victory and success and shows us that we should believe in our destination.

Sigel

Sigel is the rune of victory, success and overcoming challenges.

17
The Story of Tir

HE SAT by the fire, deep in thought, sharpening his broadsword. The firelight glinted, shining on the metal blade as he worked. Nearby, in the shadows, sat his wife and two small children, a son and a daughter. Huddled in the dimness, they watched him as he worked; the children not really knowing what this meant but afraid anyway, the wife with great sadness in her eyes. He wondered what would become of them if he didn't come home. Theirs was a small croft, but it took the two of them to manage it with the help of the children who looked after the hens and helped their mother at home. He loved his wife and children dearly. All he ever wanted was a peaceful life, but life was hard. The raiders had come from the sea and had wreaked havoc in a nearby village. They had to be stopped; else none would sleep safely at night. The room was silent, except for the crackling of the logs on the fire and the rhythmic sound of the sword against the whetstone. What words of guidance could he offer should he not return? Worse still, he thought, what if he was not there to defend them should the raiders come here?

His mind drifted back to a time long ago when he was just a child. He remembered sitting in front of the fire in this very same house with his grandfather, fascinated by the stories that he told about battles fought and won or lost.

Suddenly, he remembered something that his grandfather had told him when he was little, about a secret hiding place where he kept "The Answers". He tried to remember what it was. It was something about sacred symbols. The more he thought, the more he remembered. In his mind's eye he began to see the signs that his grandfather had scratched into the dirt floor of their croft. He remembered too, how he always erased them after telling him a story about each symbol. He was saddened that he had forgotten those special times he had shared with the old man. He felt that his grandfather was with him now in his hour of need. So intense was the feeling that he could almost taste his presence. A sense of comfort began to overwhelm him, as he sat there, thinking quietly in the light of the fire by his family. Then, without any apparent rhyme nor reason, he rose to his feet, turned to his wife and said: "Wait there. I will be back soon," before heading out of the door.

He didn't know quite what he was doing, but he began to slowly walk round the rough walls of his home. "I know they are here somewhere," he thought to himself. He sat down on the grass with his back to the stout stone wall and began again to remember those times he spent as a child in the company of the old man. It was then he realised that something was pressing into his back. He moved a little to make himself more comfortable. As before, he felt the same sensation of something pressing between his shoulder blades. He leaned forward, inclining his head trying to see what it was. He turned round further then ran his hand over the wall, for he could not see anything that obviously protruding. Then, like a bolt from the blue, realisation dawned on him. This was the very spot. He was sure of it; this is where he had seen his grandfather hide things. He took out his knife and he began to scrape around the stone he was convinced was the right one. He cleared away years of moss and soon was able to move it. His heart was hammering in his chest as the stone began to slip out of its resting place. He placed it reverently on the ground beside him and peered into the dark space. He could see nothing.

Cautiously he put his hand into the hole and began to feel around the cavity. There was nothing there!

He was stunned, he felt sure that he would find something. He sat back on his knees facing the wall. He knelt up again and once more put his hand into the space. Right at the very back of the hole there was a small ridge. Running his fingers over it, he realised that behind it lay a shallow pit. He could feel something soft lying there. Carefully he withdrew a piece of old leather, bound several times with twine. He slowly untied it, thinking all the time that his father or grandfather may have been the last to touch this precious package. He felt close to them both. It was with a heart full of hope and a deep sense of anticipation that he un-wrapped the leather. It was filled with small stones, all of a similar size and shape. He did not look at them. He closed his eyes tightly and thought deeply about his fears; then, still without looking, he put his hand onto the stones, caressed them lovingly and finally chose one.

He opened his hand to look at it. He had chosen well. The rune was Tir, the spiritual warrior. Instantly, he was filled with confidence. He knew that all would be well and that he would return victorious. All he needed to do to ensure this was to believe that he

Tir

This is the rune of overcoming obstacles and winning in times of conflict.

18

The Story of Othel

WHERE he had been in his life in the past was not important. Where he was now was the issue. He looked deeply into himself and tried to fathom out what he wanted and where he was going from here. He felt that until he found his own place, he wouldn't truly be able to find himself.

He knew that he wanted to find a special place to live, somewhere in the country. With his limited budget, however, he believed that his dream was impossible. His passions in life were his guitar and his motorbike and he had no greater pleasure than riding his cruiser through the countryside. He worked long, hard hours, so every opportunity he found to enjoy the freedom of the open road was precious to him. Other nights he would sit with his guitar putting into music the beauty he found in his soul. His father had played in various bands and, as far back as he could remember, his dad played music old and new. As a fairly young lad, he had become proficient to the extent that his father encouraged him to play at gigs with the band. When he lost him, he lost more than just the most precious person in his life. Everything went that day – music, songs, laughter and the joy of living. It was a very long time before he picked up a guitar again and when he did, it was almost against his will. He was 25 years old by that time, and his guitar was the last thing on his mind.

One of his workmates was looking for someone to form a band with and he kept on and on at him to join him one night for a session. Later, he could remember the feeling of plugging in the amp and that was it, it all came back to him. Soon he was playing every night and then he began to write songs. The words and music just came to him, especially when he was riding his bike – a song would just dance round his head and he couldn't wait to get home and pick up his guitar and play it.

Much later, living with his sister in the city temporarily, he would come home from work late in the evening, and look longingly at his bike sitting redundant in her driveway. He would sigh and wish he had the chance to take it out on the open road again.

It was his sister who saw the advertisement first and drew his attention to it. "A place in the country," it read.

"Look," she said. "Here's something that you might be interested in. It's a park home. They are usually less expensive than traditional builds." She passed the newspaper with the advertisement in I to him and although he knew that he probably couldn't afford it, he thought it would be nice to go and see what was on offer. They made arrangements to go on the following Sunday. He was looking forward to it, but he was also reluctant to be put in a situation where he would see something that he liked but couldn't afford.

He remembered the feeling that overwhelmed him as he and his sister drove up the hill on the approach to the park. A sense of anticipation filled him and broad smile broke out on his face.

The first meeting with the owner of the park was a friendly one as she let them see the various homes available and explained to them everything that they needed to know. Before he left the park that afternoon, he knew that he had found the place where he wanted to be and could afford it. More than that, he felt as if he had just seen a glimpse of who he was – who and what he would be. Happy, that was the word he was looking for. Happy!

He had a vision of his future and a picture of his past too. He knew where he was and he knew for sure what he wanted. He could see himself sitting on the veranda, strumming his guitar, while the sun set behind the trees. He thought of his father and how he would have loved this park. The memories he held were not sad because he had lost him but proud because he had known him.

Othel

Othel is the rune that is associated with property and those things in our life that we have become because of the gifts bestowed on us by our ancestors, be they material or spiritual.

19
The Story of Beork

AS THEY walked, they chatted about what they had been up to since they last saw each other. They made an attractive pair, dark haired and tanned with the summer sun. "I had my fortune told last week," the first young woman said. "Go on then, tell me?"

"She said that a baby was strong in my cards."

"Crikey! Bet that was a bit of a shock, Is there something that you're not telling me?"

"No, nothing, it freaked me out. I have hardly slept all week worrying about it."

"Well, the last time we spoke you weren't seeing anyone. Has that changed?"

"No, I'm still not seeing anyone but, you never know, I might meet the man of my dreams and he could sweep me off my feet," she replied laughing.

"Yes, and make you pregnant in the process."

They chatted as they made their way to the superstore. This was their regular outing, Once every couple of weeks they would meet, go shopping, catch up on their news and then enjoy a bar meal together before heading for their respective homes.

As they approached the superstore, they spotted a man selling *The Big Issue*.

They made their way into the store and began to fill their trolleys. They went through the checkout at the same time and as they were leaving the store, the man selling his papers separated them.

She was loading her shopping into the boot of her car when her friend caught up. "Where did you get to?"

"I was chatting to that man selling *The Big Issue*. It's a shame isn't it?"

"What's a shame?"

"That wee dog."

"What wee dog, I don't know what you are talking about?"

"Didn't you see it? I can't believe that you walked right past it and didn't see it. The *Big Issue* man has got a cardboard box at his feet and there is a tiny wee pup lying in it. There's a baby bottle half-full of milk lying beside it, and it looks as though it has turned sour. In this heat, it will die if somebody doesn't do something about it."

Without a word, she shut the boot of her car, locked it and hurried back to the entrance of the store.

"*Big Issue?*" asked the street seller.

"No thanks, but I'll give you £5 for your dog."

"Make it a tenner and I'll throw in a paper."

She took a £10 note from her purse, handed it to him and picked up the pup.

As she reached the cars, her friend approached her: "What are you going to do now?"

"Pet shop and vet, leave your car here and come in mine so that you can hold the pup while I drive."

"Right," said her friend, as she took the sick puppy in her arms.

They had only gone a short distance when they spotted a vet's surgery. They were both relieved when a quick examination showed that although the puppy was badly dehydrated, nothing seemed to be seriously wrong. The next stop was the pet shop, where it could be spoiled with puppy food, new dishes, a nice bed and some toys for good measure.

"Well your cards came true," said her friend, "you have got your baby now."

"Oh my goodness, you're right, that's spooky."

"I suppose the passionate affair is blown now," she laughed. "What are you going to call her?"

"I'm going to call her Beork, it means life."

Much later, at home, she nursed her puppy and was amazed at the speed of its recovery. It was playful and happy and after it was fed, it settled down to sleep in its new bed. A short while later, however, it woke up and vomited all over its blanket. She guessed that it was still ill from the neglect it had suffered, so she cleaned up the mess, gave it a small drink of water and settled it back down to sleep. The following couple of days were spent trying all sorts of food, but Beork was sick every time she ate. She tried everything that she could think of and the only thing that the little puppy could keep down was beaten egg yolk. On the third day, she went back to the vet's. Everyone made a fuss of Beork, but the puppy seemed to be quite sad. When her turn came the vet asked her to describe the puppy's symptoms, only to be told. "You will have to leave your puppy here overnight because we will have to do some tests. Call tomorrow afternoon and we will give you the results." That day and night were slow to pass and all she could do was worry. The following afternoon she called the vet's.

"I am afraid that your puppy has an abnormal gullet and when she eats, only a little of the food is going into her stomach. There is no choice, she will have to have an operation, but the surgery could kill her."

"When can you operate?"

"With your permission we can slot the puppy into the next space later this afternoon. Would you like us to go ahead?"

"Yes," she replied without hesitation.

"Give us a call tomorrow morning and we will let you know how she is."

The first thing she thought of when she woke up the next day was the phone call. As soon as the surgery opened, she called them. "Can you tell me how Beork is?" she asked anxiously. But the reply was not what she had hoped.

"I am very, very sorry; Beork didn't make it through the night."

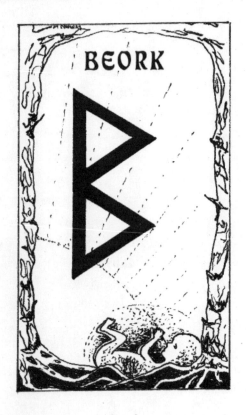

Beork

Beork or *Berkana* represents life. And not just life but the accompanying cycles of birth, life, death and rebirth. In today's society, this could represent news of a pregnancy or birth. Beork represents a fresh start, a new beginning, a recovery, a birth or a rebirth

20
The Story of Eoh

THEY sat together cross-legged on the floor in front of the fire messing around with tarot cards and rune stones, having fun and enjoying learning about the craft and the old ways, magick and dowsing. The two pretty young sisters had grown up under the influence of the wise way but hadn't, until now, paid any real attention to what they were being shown. Hocus-pocus belonging to daft old grannies who believed in superstition and magick, was how they thought of it.

"It's a sign, it's a sign," they would mimic and laugh. Theirs were travelling folk, but they had settled at this camp for some time.

When the door knocked, they almost jumped out of their skins and then they fell about giggling again. It was their friend Jamesy.

They had known him for years, but he had just come back to the area and was living nearby. It was nice to have him around again. He was a quiet boy with not much to say for himself, but he was always around when you needed a helping hand and everyone liked him. When he saw what they were up to, he too wanted to join in, but he was more in awe of the tools of divination than the girls appeared to be.

He had picked up the bag of rune stones, put his hand in and pulled one out. Jamesy turned it over to look at the mark on it. He asked the girls if they knew what it meant. The younger of the two told him that her gran believed that when that particular stone comes out, the person who drew it would be moving house.

"That's not possible," he said. "We only moved here last month."

"Well I don't know," the girl replied. "I'm only telling you what she said."

It wasn't long after that that they put the tarot cards, runes stones and dowsers away. Although they were pleased to see him, the fun had gone out of it. They couldn't have a giggle and ask about boyfriends and stuff with him there.

The next day, it was back to secondary school as usual and for the next few days nothing special happened until Jamesy arrived back at their door.

"You'll never believe what I'm going to tell you," he said. "I'm moving!"

"Oh no!" the girls replied in unison. "Where are you going? Wait a minute, that's what the rune stone said the other night!"

They all looked at each other, grinned and the three of them said together "SPOOKY!"

At first they were all laughing but the girls suddenly stopped as the realisation dawned on them that their good friend Jamesy would be moving. Their faces fell and one of them asked where he was going.

"Oh, don't worry," he replied. "The kitchen window fell out last night, so we are only moving a couple of doors down till it's fixed, I'll be around for a long while yet."

One of the girls was particularly happy to hear that for she had a crush on Jamesy and she had wondered in the past if they would be together for always.

Eoh

Traditionally this rune is known as the rune of travel, there are strong associations with marriage too.

21

The Story of Mann

MOTHER had a little white Triumph TR7, which was her pride and joy. It was really old but fairly reliable and I am sure that she loved that little car more than anything else that she had. She loved nipping in and out of town shopping or going to work in it. Her friends were very fond of it too and always looked forward to taking a ride in it.

But, if anything, I think it was me who loved that car more than anyone else did. I adored getting dropped off at school in the TR7 and being picked up again at the end of the day. And for me, the frequent trips down the coast in it were The Best. I remember one Sunday, I must have been about 12 years old and we were going for a run down the coast in the Triumph. Everything was fine and we were travelling along a stretch of dual carriageway. There were docks on one side and a rough housing scheme on the other, set about half a mile back from the road. Just as we were nearing another roundabout, the car suddenly slowed to a stop. Mother had managed to steer it into the side of the road. "Thank goodness I took out roadside assistance with my insurance," she said as she fished around in her bag for her mobile phone, only to discover that there was no signal.

We sat there a moment or two both thinking the same thing. "What now?" This was not an ideal place to be stranded. The chances of anyone stopping for us were pretty slim. We could see the large roundabout a half-mile or so ahead of us and knew that in the other direction, the only break in the dual carriageway was another roundabout two miles behind us. Mother got out of the car, lifted the bonnet and started prodding and poking at the engine. I thought that this was a waste of time because she didn't know anything about engines anyway. She left the bonnet open and got back into the car. "Maybe someone will take pity on us and stop to lend a hand," said Mother.

"Maybe some nutcase will stop and murder us," said I, scared but still hopeful that help would come. I don't know how long we sat there before Mother finally came to a decision. "Right, this is what we are going to do. We are going to lock up the car and walk to the nearest service station," she said. No sooner were the words out of her mouth, than a sleek shiny new sports car drew up in front of us. We both looked at each other, then at the handsome man who was walking towards us.

"You stay in the car and keep the door locked," said Mother as she quickly got out of the TR7.

"Got a problem?" I heard him say. He looked under the bonnet for a few minutes and then went back to his own car. Mother was obviously nervous, glanced at me and gestured that I should stay where I was. A moment later, he came back with a few tools in his hand and while he tinkered with the engine, mother thanked him for stopping and mentioned that it was lucky he had been travelling in the same direction as us.

"I wasn't," he said. " I was going the other way, but I had two miles to think about you and your passenger left here stranded and my conscience wouldn't let me go on, so I turned back at the big roundabout."

He got us started and followed us for a few miles to make sure that the car was running OK before giving us a few hoots on his horn and a cheery wave as he passed us. Mother put the TR7 into the garage for repairs and soon sold it for a newer, more reliable car. Although I was sorry to see it go, I was glad that we wouldn't be stuck in the middle of nowhere again. Much later, I remember talking to Mother about the kind man who had rescued us that day and how we had to trust him.

Mann

Mann or *Mannaz* stands for trust and indicates a person around you that you can share a secret with or trust in some way.

22
The Story of Lagu

H E HAD been so angry when it all fell apart. He stormed off, rage boiling up inside him. Soon he found himself at his favourite spot on the shore. He climbed onto the rocks, wrenched the ring off his finger and tried to throw it into the water, but he fumbled and, as the gold band flew from his hand, it spun and landed in the water not far from him. "Damn," he thought. He had wanted it out of his sight, but he could see it glistening in the water quite clearly. He immediately regretted what he had done. Now he wanted the ring back and he wanted it badly. The wind was blowing fiercely about him and the waves had begun to crash close to the top of the rocks where he was standing. There was no way that he could get the ring back; attempting to do so would probably be the end of him. Emotion welled up inside him and gradually spilled over. Tears streamed down his face and for a little while he could fool himself and blame the sea spray for the dampness. Soon it was dark and he had no choice but to go home. Home! It would never be the same.

The next day, he went back to the rocks. He was amazed to see that the ring was still lodged in the stones, but it was too dangerous to try to reach it. He cursed himself for being so stupid. He wanted that ring back and he tormented himself with how he was going to get it.

He sat there a long time thinking, just thinking. Much later, he sadly made his way home. In the days that followed, all he could think about was the ring and how he could get it back. Each day he went to the rocks and each time the ring sparkled and taunted him for his stupidity. The sea spray washed his face and, although he did not know it, all of this was part of his healing-learning process. He soon began to notice that, as the days went on, the tide was getting lower and lower. The penny dropped. All he had to do was be on the rocks when the tide was at its lowest.

Back home, he searched the telephone directory for the address of ship chandlers. Finding one close by, he bought a tide table and a pair of waders. All the way home, he was smiling to himself. That night, he studied the tide table and rising very early the next morning, he dressed and made his way to the shore.

The tide was out as he clambered on to the rocks that were nearest to where the ring was lodged. But it was still hopeless; he slipped, slithered and stretched with all his might, but he still couldn't reach the ring. One last attempt, he decided, and if he didn't get it, he would go back home and try again the next day. "Argh," he roared as he slipped and fell, slamming against the rocks. Somehow he managed to catch a hold and he pulled himself up. He didn't get the ring but he had given himself a fright and a good soaking.

He decided that he would give it one last try another day, and if he didn't get it, he would give up. The next morning, off he went on his mission. He lay across the nearest rock and stretched for all his worth. He could feel the ring in his fingers but it was difficult to prize it free. Suddenly, he had it and just as suddenly he was in the water, fighting for his life. The current was pulling him away and then slamming him back against the rocks. The ring was the last thing on his mind now. All he could think of was survival. Waves crashed over him and he could see glimpses of light and rocks as he tumbled and twisted in the water. His waders quickly filled up with water and made it difficult, if not impossible, for him to stay afloat, never mind swim. In the next moment, he caught hold of a rock and held on for all his might. Inch by inch, he pulled himself to safety and as he lay there on the top of the rocks panting and coughing, he wondered momentarily what he had been thinking of, risking his life and sanity over a damn ring.

When he had recovered sufficiently, he carefully made his way back off the rocks and walked forlornly across the shore to his car. He dragged off his waders and threw them into the boot of his car in disgust. He was cold now and shivering. All he wanted was to get home and to get dry. He was not aware of the drive back but he got there. The first thing he did was to put the kettle on to make a cup of tea. He stood in the kitchen waiting for it to boil and stripped off his soaking clothes. Tea made, he went into the bathroom and ran a hot bath. He ached all over and his hands were covered in cuts from the beating that he had experienced when thrown repeatedly against the rocks. Bruises were beginning to appear on his arms and legs and he realised that he was very lucky to have survived.

He dried off, went straight to bed and slept the sleep of the exhausted for a long time. When he eventually rose, he went to the kitchen to clear up his wet clothes, which were still lying in a pile where he had dropped them. The kitchen floor was wet with seawater and he mopped this up as best he could, and threw the clothes into the washing machine. He made himself lunch and sat down to enjoy it as the machine ran its cycle. Lunch over and feeling a little better, he went about his business.

Even though he had promised himself that he wouldn't, he went back to the shore. He could not believe it! The tide was so far out that the rock where the ring had been was completely exposed and, if he had wanted to, he could have easily reached it without any danger. In spite of himself, he scanned the surrounding area, but there was no sign of the ring. Later, after he had gone home, he began to empty the washing machine and as he shook out his clothes, something tinkled to the floor. He felt a rumble in the pit of his stomach as the laughter began to build in him. He stood there laughing and crying at the same time as he looked at the ring lying at his feet. It must have become trapped in his clothes during his struggle for life. What a lesson to learn. He had almost killed himself trying to get what he wanted and all he had to do was wait and it would have been his.

Lagu

This rune encompasses the element of water and deals with our emotions. It teaches us to wait rather than to force issues in an attempt to have what we want before the time is right.

23

The Story of Ing

THE training had been hard and, while he knew that it would be, he had been unlucky too and sprains and strains had taken their toll and delayed his progress. All he could think about was coming first and he had made a promise to himself that no matter what it took, he would do everything in his power to win. He had never been interested in running or competing before the car crash. But the memory of the accident was vivid: he was hanging upside down, trapped by his seatbelt and thinking that he would never get out alive. The emergency services were quick to arrive at the scene of the smash and it took them over an hour to cut him free.

His injuries were horrific. He spent months in hospital recovering and he could still hear the consultant's voice ringing in his ears, telling him that he might never walk again. He knew that he would, but he could still feel the fear that perhaps the surgeons would be right. He knew something that the surgeons didn't know and his secret gave him the strength to overcome anything. He had only told one person about his secret because he was convinced that people would think he was crazy.

Thinking back to the accident, he could remember standing beside someone, looking at the car surrounded by emergency vehicles. He could see it all quite clearly. The fire engine, the paramedics, the ambulance and the police were all there, as he and the man stood chatting. He couldn't remember actually seeing the man's face, but he could recall their conversation. The man seemed to be urging him to hurry up, while he was telling the man to look at the guy that the emergency services were trying to cut free. "You better hurry. You don't have much time," the man urged.

Suddenly, he became aware that not only was he the person outside the car watching the events, he was also the person inside the car experiencing them. The next moment, he was back in the car feeling the agonising pain from his injuries and fearing that he might die there on the road. The man was nowhere to be seen. Much later, in hospital, he had plenty of time to think about his out-of-body experience and he realised that there was a much more powerful force, a God a

Something, that was helping him. That's when he found the will to beat the odds.

His feet were on the starting blocks and the starter pistol sounded in his ears. He took off and ran for all his might. A feeling of joy washed over him and he felt as though he was flying. There was no one in front of him and he led the way right to the end of the track. He could hear the cheers of the spectators and suddenly he felt himself being lifted, hoisted high onto the shoulders of his close friends who had run onto the track to congratulate him. He'd won! He had beaten the odds and every pain, every effort, every struggle had been worth it, because now it had all come together.

Ing

Ing or *Inguz* teaches us that effort brings reward and, more especially, Ing shows us that we *will* experience the greatest reward.

24

The Story of Daeg

E ACH and every day was an effort. He felt that no matter what he did, or tried to do, his progress was blocked or thwarted in some way. He felt hopeless. At first his friends offered support and encouragement but, as the days turned into weeks and the weeks turned into months, one by one they had drifted away until there was no one but himself. At first when he lost his job, he would rise early in the morning and go to the Job Centre, picking up the daily paper on his way. He would scan the pages looking for work. To begin with, he was searching for something that he would enjoy doing and that would pay him well. Later, he was just looking for any old job. It seemed that no one wanted to employ him.

He had been good at what he was trained to do, but an earlier injury meant that he couldn't go back to that line of work. Some companies at least had the decency to write back to him, letting him know that he had not been successful in his application, but the majority didn't bother and he found that difficult to deal with. He hated signing on and collecting state benefits, but he couldn't survive without them. The depression crept up on him gradually and at first he just lay in bed a little longer than usual. As time went on, he began to spend more and more time in bed. Some days he only got up to have a cup of tea and to eat.

He could look back on that horrible time now and remember with clarity the day that everything changed for him. He had risen very late and made his way to the kitchen to put the kettle on. There was a letter lying on the floor by the front door. It looked important. It was a large envelope with a company logo on it. He picked it up and looked at it on both sides. He dreaded opening it for he was sure that it was another disappointment, another refusal. He looked at the address of the sender and it took some time for him to remember which job he had applied for that it related to.

He sat the letter on the kitchen table whilst he drank his tea. The longer he delayed opening it, the further away the disappointment would be. Eventually he picked up a kitchen knife, slipped the blade below the flap and opened it. He couldn't believe his luck. It was a job offer and he had to go for an informal interview the following day just to make final arrangements for training and a start date. He remembered the enthusiasm he felt as he ran upstairs to his wardrobe to make sure that he had clean shirt and suit. He looked in the mirror and decided that he looked awful, but a haircut, shower and shave would make all the difference.

That was six months ago, and he still felt the same enthusiasm every day when his alarm clock sounded, letting him know that it was time to get up for work. He could define that feeling quite clearly in his mind as he looked at the man sitting in front of him now, asking for a job. It was hope and without that all you have is hopelessness. He knew what that felt like and with that thought offered the applicant a job on the spot.

Daeg

Daeg shows us that there is some opportunity or opening ahead that will give us a reason to look forward. Daeg shows us hope for the future.

25
The Story of Wyrd

'I CANNOT deal with this right now," she thought to herself. She had just received a letter from an old friend, telling her that she would be coming to see her later that day. She was annoyed about this because when they had last seen each other, they had not parted on good terms. She had felt used and she did not like that feeling. Moreover, she had no intentions of allowing it to happen again. She even began to wonder if the letter had been timed so that she would be unable to make an excuse to postpone the visit. She was not going to be fooled by that one. She had things to do before she could leave the house, but if she hurried, she would manage to get through everything and go before the visitor arrived.

She felt as though she had enough to deal with at this time without having to face an unwanted confrontation on top of everything else. Watching the clock, she hurried through her day's tasks. The letter said the woman would be coming at 2pm, and it was only 11am now, so she had plenty of time to attend to what had to be done. Working from home had its advantages, but there were drawbacks too and situations like this being forced on her could be described as one of them. The phone rang several times while she was working, delaying her, but eventually at 12.45pm she was ready to go. She put on fresh lipstick, brushed her hair picked up her briefcase, car keys and jacket, and made her way to the front door.

Just as she reached it, the doorbell rang. As she opened the door, her mouth dropped open in dismay as she recognised the visitor she had been so determined to avoid. The woman was carrying a beautiful bunch of flowers. "Don't panic," she said. "I have just come to say a few words and then I will go. I treated you badly the last time we saw each other and I cannot forgive myself for it. I know these flowers won't make up for that, but I saw them and knew you would like them. Please forgive me. I miss your friendship and if you can forgive me I would appreciate a second chance. If not, I will understand." At that her friend handed over the flowers and turned to walk away. "Wait!" she cried. "Come in and we can have a chat."

Wyrd

Wyrd shows us that no matter how hard you try to manipulate destiny you will not succeed. What will be, will be. Wyrd is the "inevitable" rune.

General Guidance

Using three runes

Prepare yourself and your surroundings to set the mood. Concentrate on what you are about to do and, when you are ready, spread all your runes face down. Think of your life as it is at this time and, in your mind, ask for guidance. Choose your runes in the following order:

First rune
This rune shows your immediate situation.

Second rune
This symbol points to an obstacle or opportunity.

Third rune
This shows the likely outcome if the obstacle is avoided or the opportunity taken.

Sample interpretation number one

First rune: Mann

This symbol is telling you that there is someone around you that you can share special times with. This person will be honest with you and you can depend on him or her.

Second rune: Geofu

A promise or proposal will be made to you. This could be a business or romantic opportunity.

Third rune: Feoh

If you accept the offer made, it will lead to financial security and prosperity.

Sample interpretation number two

First rune: Rad

Someone who has come from some distance or who is connected to travel or transport will, make an appearance in your life. This person has a hidden agenda and caution should be exercised.

Second rune: Ken

An offer will be made to you or an opening will appear that you may want to take advantage of.

Third rune: Nied

If you proceed at this time, you will have many regrets. Be patient. Examine the small print and take care that you do not act in haste. Problems lie ahead.

General guidance using rune stones

Sit quietly, holding your bag of rune stones. Think of your life as it is today. When you feel as though you are ready, close your eyes and put your hand into your rune bag. Draw out three runes. Without looking at them, place them on the mat in front of you and then open your eyes and look at the symbols you have chosen.

Sample interpretation number one

First rune stone: Tir (upright)

This symbol shows you that you will have to stand up for yourself. You may attend an interview or a formal meeting. Your mood should be confident and, if you show that you are confident and believe in yourself, you will win.

Second rune stone: Ur (upright)

In this position, this symbol means that you will prove yourself and overcome any obstacles.

Third rune stone: Wyrd

You are being shown that this situation or experience is unavoidable and that good fortune is on your side.

Sample interpretation number two

First rune stone: Hagall (upright)

Sudden changes will upset your plans or disrupt your life in some way.

Second rune stone: Is

You are being warned to take no action at this time.

Third rune stone: Beork (upright)

The outcome will be positive in spite of your fears and doubts. Be patient and you will see that you are being given a chance to recover from your difficulties or to start again.

Horoscope spread

The horoscope spread is a layout consisting of 13 positions, or houses, with each house governed by a sign of the zodiac. Each sign governs a certain aspect of our life; consequently, this type of spread will address every area of our life.

You will lay the cards out in a circle, like a clock, with one in the centre. This layour is explained later in this section

The houses

First house: matters affecting you today

Ruled by Aries, this house relates to what is currently around you, how you feel and, what you can expect in the very near future. Physical appearance can be reflected in this house, particularly matters concerning the head and face.

Second house: money matters

Ruled by Taurus, this house relates to all financial affairs and those aspects that will influence them. When you are reading the rune in this house, it is always advisable to also look at the rune that is in the sixth house, which relates to career matters. Both houses should be read together to give a deeper understanding of the issues shown. This house also represents the ears, nose, throat and neck.

Third house: family matters and incoming news

Ruled by Gemini, this house will show you information pertaining to your family and incoming news. Creative projects and anything to do with papers may be shown here too. This house also represents the lungs, arms, hands and shoulders.

Fourth house: matters in and close to home

Ruled by Cancer, this house relates to how things are, or will develop in or around your home. Property and savings or investments are shown here as well as fathers or father figures. This house also represents the digestive system and the chest.

Fifth house: social and romantic interests

Ruled by Leo, your love life and good times, or lack of them, will be shown here. You may also be shown opportunities and things to avoid or take advantage of, as well as social plans or holidays. This house also represents the heart and back.

Sixth house: matters concerning occupation and health
Ruled by Virgo, this house relates to work opportunities, changes that may occur, difficulties around the workplace and any matters pertaining to general health and wellbeing. Always look at the rune that is in the second house when reading this one to assess the financial implications. Information regarding small domestic animals can be found here. The sixth house also represents the stomach and digestive organs.

Seventh house: personal and business partnerships
Ruled by Libra, the rune in this position relates to committed relationships and partnerships of any kind, be it business or pleasure. Marriage or divorce, reconciliations and legal affairs will be shown here too. This house also represents the kidneys and veins.

Eighth house: new beginnings and endings
Ruled by Scorpio, here you will be informed about situations or events in your life, which are ending or beginning. This can be physical, emotional or spiritual. Rumours, gossip or slander may be indicated here as well as spiritual studies. This house also represents the sex organs and the bladder.

Ninth house: education and travel

Ruled by Sagittarius, this is where you will be given advice relating to situations or events, which are connected to travel or transport. This can be because you will or will not be making a journey of some description, or it may relate to an experience that you will encounter while travelling or away from home. In addition, the rune in this position, will be relating to events occurring around someone you know who lives some distance away from you. Matters relating to universities and colleges, schools and students may be shown here. This house also represents the thighs, hips, liver and nervous system.

Tenth house: hopes for the future and ambitions

Ruled by Capricorn, this house will show you what you are currently hoping for, even if it is a secret desire. Your reputation and social standing will be reflected in this position and reference may be made to your mother and your superiors in the workplace. When a negative rune appears here, you are being shown that hopes have been dashed.

This house also represents the knees.

Eleventh house: social circle

Ruled by Aquarius, here you will be shown situations that relate to people you know, but who are not related to you. It is this house that points to information regarding groups, clubs or organisations that you may be a member of. It also represents the lower legs and the ankles.

Twelfth house: fears and anxieties

Ruled by Pisces, this house is sometimes known as the house of secrets and where the 10th house shows your hopes and dreams, this one shows your deepest fears. When a positive rune appears here, you are being advised that your fears are unfounded or you have passed the worst.

The 12th house also represents the feet and the toes.

Thirteenth house: overriding influence

This house has no ruling planet, as it can represent you or an influence that will affect your life. This influence can be a person or a situation. The rune that sits in this position is probably one of the most important; it will show whether the time span covered by the reading will be an easy or difficult one. If the rune in this house is a negative one, then there will be a negative undercurrent or influence running through all events. If, on the other hand, the rune is a positive one, then the influence or undercurrent will be positive. What we are really hoping to see here is a good rune.

Casting a horoscope spread

Prepare yourself as before and if you are using rune stones, hold your bag or box of runes in your hands whilst you think about your life. When you are ready, take one rune at a time and lay the first face down in the centre position, position 13, on your mat. Now begin to lay the next 12 runes face up as follows: beginning at the nine o'clock position (position one), and working anti-clockwise, place the next rune in position two (eight o'clock) and the remaining runes in positions three (seven o'clock), four (six o'clock), etc, until all 13 spaces (houses) have a rune in them. When you have laid out your 12th rune, you may then turn over the one in the 13th house.

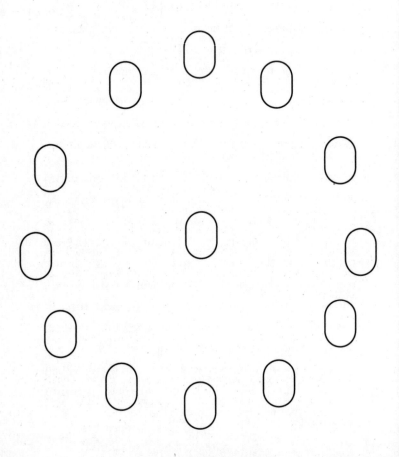

The Horoscope Spread

Sample interpretation

First house: matters affecting you today
Beork (upright)

A new beginning is indicated within the coming four weeks. There may be news of the recovery of someone after an illness or a fresh start after a difficult period. News of a pregnancy or birth may also be forthcoming.

Second house: money matters
Eoh (reversed)

Travel plans may be delayed or cancelled and caution should be exercised. Because of this, money should not be spent at this time on anything to do with travel or transport.

Third house: family matters and incoming news
Sigel

This is the rune of victory and success, so good news is on the way and the outcome of a situation will be very favourable.

Fourth house: matters in and close to home
Ken (upright)

An opening or offer will be made. This offer will mean

that you will have much to do should you accept. Bear in mind that Ken represents fire and, therefore, if you act without thought and consideration, you could have your fingers burned. If the surrounding runes are positive then you have nothing to worry about.

Fifth house: social and romantic interests
Wynn (reversed)

In this position, the omens are not good and care should be exercised. Do not put all your eggs in one basket as plans could fail.

Sixth house: matters concerning occupation and health
Peorth (upright)

In this position, you are being told that there is information that you are not aware of relevant to your situation. You will be given these details in due course, but not until destiny is ready.

Seventh house: personal and business partnerships
Jara (upright)

When this rune appears, you are being told that you will reap the benefits of your efforts. The harder you work, the greater will be the rewards. The period referred to can be as little as one day or as great as one year.

Eighth house: new beginnings and endings
Geofu

Gefu represents a promise or commitment being made to you, or by you, to another. Contracts may be signed pertaining to business matters and weddings or engagements will be significant.

Ninth house: education and travel
Thorn (upright)

In this position, you are being advised that an opportunity may suddenly appear. This opportunity must be handled with extreme care to avoid upsetting a positive outcome.

Tenth house: hopes for the future and ambitions
Eolh (reversed)

You are treading on dangerous ground and are being advised that it is not safe for you to continue with a current plan or course of action.

Eleventh house: social circle
Ur (reversed)

Since this position is associated with friends and colleagues, the advice given may indeed be pertinent to their influence or connection to a business matter, or the advice may be given relating to their situation. Ur indicates that, at this time, one should not speculate in matters of business, finance or legalities, or indeed anything in which there is a challenge to overcome.

Twelfth house: fears and anxieties
Ansur (reversed)

You are afraid that there will be delays or cancellations. Communication may bring problems and there may be faults with telephone lines, modems or mail-delivery services. If involved with face-to-face meetings, be careful not to say more than you mean to.

Thirteenth house: overriding influence
Mann (upright)

This is an indication that there is a person around you that you can share a secret with or trust in some way. Perhaps he or she will be there to help or support you when you most need them. This person can be regarded as a good friend.

Short Interpretations

One: Feoh

Upright

In this position Feoh represents an increase of wealth or financial income and bodes well for speculation in business or financial matters.

Reversed

This represents financial loss. Do not borrow or lend and do not speculate at this time.

Two: Ur

Upright

In today's society, this could represent an interview for a new job, taking a driving test or any other event that will in some way be challenging, testing and life changing. Ur indicates overcoming obstacles and having a successful outcome to a challenge.

Reversed

Ur, in this position, represents failure and insurmountable odds. At this time, do not speculate in matters of business, finance or legalities or, indeed, anything in which there is a challenge to overcome.

Three: Thorn

Upright

In this position, you are being advised that an opportunity may suddenly appear. This opportunity must be handled with extreme care to avoid upsetting a positive outcome.

Reversed

Proceed with extreme caution and at your peril. This is an indication that matters may not have a successful outcome.

Four: Ansur

Upright

Letters, telephone calls and communication of all kinds will be important to you. Communication is the key here, and listening is every bit as important as speaking. If you have something that you are holding back on, talk about it; and if someone tells you that you are not listening, pay attention.

Reversed

You can expect all kinds of communication break-downs from face-to-face meetings being cancelled to faults with telephone lines, modems or mail-delivery services. If involved with a face-to-face situation, be careful not to say more than you mean to.

Five: Rad

Upright

Rad, in this position, represents a journey being made by you or by someone who is coming towards you. The outcome of this trip cannot be depended upon and may end in a very different way from that which you anticipate. There are hidden agendas that you may, or may not, be aware of. Do not pin your hopes on an anticipated outcome.

Reversed

Rad reversed represents plans being rearranged at the last minute or even cancelled. You may meet someone new who, though likeable, cannot be trusted. Be careful!

Six: Ken

Upright

In this position, Ken speaks of an opening or offer that will be made. This offer will mean that you will have much to do, should you accept. Bear in mind that Ken represents fire and, therefore, if you act without thought and consideration, you could have your fingers burned.

Reversed

The omens are not good when Ken appears in this position. You are being warned not to accept or become involved in something that is being offered.

Seven: Gefu

Gefu represents a promise or commitment being made to you, or by you, to another. This can be relating to friendship, love, or business. Since this symbol is the same no matter which way it falls, other runes chosen in the company of this one will say whether the promise is based on the truth or a lie and whether you should believe it or not.

Eight: Wynn

Upright

This is the rune that will bring great happiness to any question, situation, or person. Success is indicted in career. and business matters. Travel and matters connected to transport, will bring added benefits.

Reversed

In this position, the omens are not good and care should be exercised. Do not put all your eggs in one basket, as plans could fail.

Nine: Hagall

Upright

In this position, Hagall represents a sudden unex-pected change. It can be likened to sudden hailstorms that appear out of nowhere and are gone almost as quickly as they begin. This type of change can be ben-eficial, but it is always better to have a "Plan B" to fall back on.

Reversed

The omens are not good when Hagall appears reversed. Do not make any plans or take any chances, as the signs are ominous.

10: Nied

Upright

Nied represents an obstruction or obstacle in your life or in a given situation. Forcing your will against this obstruction will only bring tears.

Reversed

In this position, Nied is issuing a warning to you that you will experience grief or discomfort. Be careful in everything that you do.

11: Is

Whether upright or reversed, the Is symbol is the same and is warning you to stand still, take no action, make no changes. This rune may also be advising you that plans may be cancelled due to unforeseen circumstances or unexpected changes.

Position 12: Jara

This rune, which is the same upright or reversed, is known as the rune of harvest. In other words, when it appears, you are being told that you will reap the benefits of your efforts. The harder you work, the greater will be the rewards. The period referred to can be as little as one day or as great as one year.

13: Yr

This rune, sometimes known as Eiwaz and referring to Yggdrasil, a yew tree, the tree of all trees, the centre of all creation. The rune means the same upright or reversed, and is known as the rune of continuous effort. In other words, when it appears, there is a project underway that requires sustained hard work to bring rewards.

14: Peorth

Upright

In this position, you are being told that there is information that you are not aware of that is relevant to your situation. You will be given this information in due course but not until destiny is ready.

Reversed

This indicates that secrets are being hidden from you. Be careful whom you trust with your secrets or they may be revealed without your knowledge or approval.

15: Eolh

Upright

This is the rune of protection, so regardless of your situation, you are being advised that you are safe to proceed on your course or plan of action.

Reversed

You are treading on dangerous ground and are being warned that it is not safe for you to continue with a current plan or course of action.

16: Sigel

This is the rune of victory and success and the outcome will be very favourable. As there is no reverse interpretation for this symbol, other runes chosen in the company of Sigel will say whether the promise is based on the truth or a lie, and whether you should believe it or not.

17: Tir

Upright

Tir is the spiritual warrior and gives courage to your spirit and to your present or forthcoming situation. Know you will be successful, and at the end of the day, regardless of the outcome, you will be – even if you do not realise this at the time.

Reversed

The forecast is not good when Tir appears in the reversed position because you will not be successful in your endeavours.

18: Othel

Upright

Matters concerning the home or property will be significant. Your integrity as a person may be put to the test, but the outcome is promising.

Reversed

Property matters may bring disappointments. Be careful if asked to sign documents.

19: Beork

Upright

Beork indicates an end and a new beginning. It can predict the recovery of someone after an illness or a fresh start following a difficult period.

Reversed

Beork represents a loss. This can be of confidence, property, face, life, courage, or indeed failing in some venture or plan.

20: Eoh

Upright

Traditionally this rune is known as the rune of travel, the kind of travel that is associated with moving home. There are strong associations with marriage, probably because of the connection between this and the setting up of a new home. Indications associated with this rune advise us to trust in destiny, for it is she who knows all there is to know about us.

Reversed

Travel plans may be delayed or cancelled and caution should be exercised.

21: Mann

Upright

This is an indication that there is a person around you that you can share a secret with or trust. Perhaps this person will help or support you in some way. Whatever happens, they can be regarded as a good friend.

Reversed

Be careful and do not believe everything that you hear. Someone around you is not to be trusted.

22: Lagu

Upright

You are being cautioned to wait for things to come to you or develop, rather than trying to force a desired outcome.

Reversed

Caution is being warned here. Emotional turmoil will be the outcome.

23: Ing

Ing is the same, whichever way it falls, and teaches us that effort brings reward and that we are being blessed with a positive outcome.

24: Daeg

Another symbol which is the same, upright or reversed, Daeg indicates that an opportunity or opening lies ahead that will relieve worries and give reason to look forward with hope for the future.

25: Wyrd

This means simply that the outcome or situation connected to the question asked is inevitable.

Name and Numerology

Boy's name	Rune symbols	Rune numbers	Total	Key number	Key word
Alan		32370	15	6	Abundance
Alasdair		32311339	25	7	Courage
Albert		3234930	24	6	Abundance
Alder		321490	19	1	Victory
Aldis		321310	10	1	Victory
Aldo		3214	10	1	Victory
Aldrich		32193300	21	3	Fertility
Alec		3243	12	3	Fertility
Aled		32410	10	1	Victory
Alexander		3245371490	38	2	Friendship
Alf		326	11	2	Friendship
Alfred		3269410	25	7	Courage
Alister		32313490	25	7	Courage
Allan		32237	17	8	Dedication
Alphonse		322047140	23	5	Caution
Alvin		32137	16	7	Courage

Book of Runes

Boy's name	Rune symbols	Rune numbers	Total	Key number	Key word
Amadeus	ᛗᛗᚱᛝᛗᛝᛋ	32314710	21	3	Fertility
Ambrose	ᛗᛗᛒᚱᛩᛋᛗ	3239414	26	8	Dedication
Amerigo	ᛗᛗᛗᚱᛁᚷᛩ	3249364	31	4	Stability
Amery	ᛗᛗᛗᚱᛋ	32498	26	8	Dedication
Andreas	ᛋᚼᛝᚱᛗᛝᛋ	3719431	28	1	Victory
Andrew	ᛋᚼᛝᚱᛗᛈ	371941	25	7	Courage
Angus	ᛋᚼᚷᛝᛋ	37671	24	6	Abundance
Anthony	ᛋᚼᛏᛚᛩᚼᛋ	3730478	32	5	Caution
Anton	ᛋᚼᛏᛩᚼ	37347	24	6	Abundance
Archibald	ᚱᚲᛚᛒᛗᛝᛞ	3930333210	27	9	Accomplishment
Argyle	ᚱᚱᚷᛚᛗᛗ	396824	32	5	Caution
Ariel	ᚱᚱᛁᛗᛏ	393420	21	3	Fertility
Armand	ᚱᚱᛗᚼᛝᛞ	3923710	25	7	Courage
Armstrong	ᚱᚱᛗᛋᛏᚱᛩᚼᚷ	3921394760	44	8	Dedication
Arnold	ᚱᚱᚼᛩᛞᛞ	397421	26	8	Dedication
Arthur	ᚱᚱᛏᚾᚾᚱ	393079	31	4	Stability
Arturo	ᚱᚱᛏᚾᚱᛩ	393794	35	8	Dedication
Auberon	ᛗᛒᛗᚱᛩᚼ	3734947	37	1	Victory
Augustus	ᛗᚷᛝᛋᛏᛝᛋ	37671371	35	8	Dedication
Bailey	ᛒᛝᛗᛗᛋ	333248	23	5	Caution
Baird	ᛒᛝᚱᛞ	333910	19	1	Victory
Baldric	ᛒᛝᛞᛞᚱᚲ	3321933	24	6	Abundance
Baldwin	ᛒᛝᛞᛞᛈᚼ	33211370	20	2	Friendship
Balfour	ᛒᛝᛚᛈᛩᚾᚱ	3326479	34	7	Courage
Barlow	ᛒᛝᚱᛋᛩᛈ	3392410	22	4	Stability
Barnum	ᛒᚱᚼᛝᛗ	3397720	31	4	Stability

Boy's name	*Rune symbols*	*Rune numbers*	*Total*	*Key number*	*Key word*
Barry	ᛒᚨᚱᚱᛇ	339980	32	5	Caution
Bart	ᛒᚨᚱᛏ	3393	18	9	Accomplishment
Basil	ᛒᚨᛊᛁᛚ	331320	12	3	Fertility
Bauldric	ᛒᚨᚢᛚᛞᚱᛁᚲ	33719330	29	2	Friendship
Baxter	ᛒᚨᚦᛏᛖᚱ	3353490	27	9	Accomplishment
Beau	ᛒᛖᚨᚢ	34370	17	8	Dedication
Bededict	ᛒᛖᛞᛖᛞᛁᚲᛏ	34141333	22	4	Stability
Ben	ᛒᛖᚾ	347	14	5	Caution
Benjamin	ᛒᛖᚾᛃᚨᛗᛁᚾ	34783237	37	1	Victory
Bennet	ᛒᛖᚾᚾᛖᛏ	347743	28	1	Victory
Benson	ᛒᛖᚾᛊᛟᚾ	3471470	26	8	Dedication
Bernard	ᛒᛖᚱᚾᚨᚱᛞ	34973910	36	9	Accomplishment
Billie	ᛒᛁᛚᛚᛖ	3322340	17	8	Dedication
Bing	ᛒᛁᚾᚷ	33760	19	1	Victory
Birch	ᛒᛁᚱᚲᚺ	339300	18	9	Accomplishment
Björn	ᛒᛃᛟᚱᚾ	380970	27	9	Accomplishment
Blair	ᛒᛚᚨᛁᚱ	32339	20	2	Friendship
Blake	ᛒᛚᚨᚲᛖ	323340	15	6	Abundance
Bob	ᛒᛟᛒ	343	10	1	Victory
Booth	ᛒᛟᛟᛏᚺ	344300	14	5	Caution
Boris	ᛒᛟᚱᛁᛊ	349310	20	2	Friendship
Bowie	ᛒᛟᚹᛁᛖ	341340	15	6	Abundance
Bradford	ᛒᚱᚨᛞᚠᛟᚱᛞ	393164910	36	9	Accomplishment
Bradley	ᛒᚱᚨᛞᛚᛖᛇ	39312480	30	3	Fertility
Brandon	ᛒᚱᚨᚾᛞᛟᚾ	39371470	34	7	Courage
Brendan	ᛒᚱᛖᚾᛞᚨᚾ	39471370	34	7	Courage

Book of Runes

Boy's name	Rune symbols	Rune numbers	Total	Key number	Key word
Brent	ᛒᚱᛖᛗᛏᛏ	394730	26	8	Dedication
Brian	ᛒᚱᛁᚨᛏ	393370	25	7	Courage
Broderic	ᛒᚱᛟᛞᛖᚱᛁᚲ	39414933	36	9	Accomplishment
Bruce	ᛒᚱᚢᚲᛖ	39734	26	8	Dedication
Bryn	ᛒᚱᛁᛏ	39870	27	9	Accomplishment
Burt	ᛒᚢᚱᛏ	37930	22	4	Stability
Byron	ᛒᛁᚱᛟᛏ	38947	31	4	Stability
Cain	ᚲᚨᛏ	33370	16	7	Courage
Callisto	ᚲᚨᛚᛚᛁᛋᛏᛟ	332231340	21	3	Fertility
Calum	ᚲᚨᛚᛗ	33272	17	8	Dedication
Cameron	ᚲᚨᛗᛖᚱᛟᛏ	33249470	32	5	Caution
Casey	ᚲᚨᛋᛖᛁ	33148	19	1	Victory
Cecil	ᚲᛖᚲᛁᛚ	34332	15	6	Abundance
Cedric	ᚲᛖᛞᚱᛁᚲ	341933	23	5	Caution
Charles	ᚲᚺᚨᚱᛚᛖᛋ	30392410	22	4	Stability
Chester	ᚲᚺᛖᛋᛏᛖᚱ	30413490	24	6	Abundance
Chris	ᚲᚺᚱᛁᛋ	309310	16	7	Courage
Christian	ᚲᚺᚱᛁᛋᛏᛁᚨᛏ	3093133370	32	5	Caution
Christopher	ᚲᚺᚱᛁᛋᛏᛟᚲᚺᛖᚱ	309313420490	38	2	Friendship
Churchill	ᚲᚺᚢᚱᚲᚺᛁᛚ	3079303220	29	2	Friendship
Claude	ᚲᛚᚨᛞᛖ	323714	20	2	Friendship
Clayton	ᚲᛚᚨᛁᛏᛟᛏ	3238347	30	3	Fertility
Clement	ᚲᛚᛖᛗᛖᛏᛏ	3242473	25	7	Courage
Cliff	ᚲᛚᛁᚠᚠ	32366	20	2	Friendship
Clifton	ᚲᛚᛁᚠᛏᛟᛏ	3236347	28	1	Victory
Clinton	ᚲᛚᛁᛏᛏᛟᛏ	3237347	29	2	Friendship

Boy's name	Rune symbols	Rune numbers	Total	Key number	Key word
Clive	ᚲᛁᛚᚢᛖ	32314	13	4	Stability
Colin	ᚲᛟᛚᛁᚾ	34237	19	1	Victory
Conan	ᚲᛟᚾᚨᚾ	34737	24	6	Abundance
Connor	ᚲᛟᚾᚾᛟᚱ	347749	34	7	Courage
Conrad	ᚲᛟᚾᚱᚨᛞ	3479310	27	9	Accomplishment
Constantine	ᚲᛟᚾᛋᛏᚨᚾᛏᛁᚾᛖ	347133733740	45	9	Accomplishment
Cornelius	ᚲᛟᚱᚾᛖᛚᛁᚢᛋ	349742371	40	4	Stability
Courtney	ᚲᛟᚢᚱᛏᚾᛖᛦ	34793748	45	9	Accomplishment
Craig	ᚲᚱᚨᛁᚷ	393360	24	6	Abundance
Creighton	ᚲᚱᛖᛁᚷᚺᛏᛟᚾ	3943603470	39	3	Fertility
Curtis	ᚲᚢᚱᛏᛁᛋ	379331	26	8	Dedication
Cyril	ᚲᛦᚱᛁᛚ	38932	25	7	Courage
Cyrus	ᚲᛦᚱᚢᛋ	38971	28	1	Victory
Dale	ᛞᚨᛚᛖ	13240	10	1	Victory
Dalziel	ᛞᚨᛚᛦᛁᛖᛚ	13243420	19	1	Victory
Damian	ᛞᚨᛗᛁᚨᚾ	1323370	19	1	Victory
Daniel	ᛞᚨᚾᛁᛖᛚ	1373420	20	2	Friendship
Darcy	ᛞᚨᚱᚲᛦ	13938	24	6	Abundance
Darell	ᛞᚨᚱᛖᛚᛚ	1394220	21	3	Fertility
Darius	ᛞᚨᚱᛁᚢᛋ	1393710	24	6	Abundance
Darren	ᛞᚨᚱᚱᛖᚾ	139947	33	6	Abundance
Darryl	ᛞᚨᚱᚱᚱᛦᛚ	1399820	32	5	Caution
David	ᛞᚨᚢᛁᛞ	131310	9	9	Accomplishment
Dean	ᛞᚨᛖᚾ	14370	15	6	Abundance
Denis	ᛞᛖᚾᛁᛋ	14731	16	7	Courage
Denzel	ᛞᛖᚾᛦᛖᛚ	147442	22	4	Stability

Boy's name	*Rune symbols*	*Rune numbers*	*Total*	*Key number*	*Key word*
Derek	ᛞᛖᚱᛖᚲ	14943	21	3	Fertility
Dermot	ᛞᛖᚱᛗᛟᛏ	149243	23	5	Caution
Dexter	ᛞᛖᚦᛏᛖᚱ	145349	26	8	Dedication
Dick	ᛞᛁᚲᚲ	1333	10	1	Victory
Digby	ᛞᛁᚷᛒᛇ	13638	21	3	Fertility
Dillon	ᛞᛁᛚᛚᛟᚾ	132247	19	1	Victory
Dominic	ᛞᛟᛗᛁᚾᛁᚲ	1423733	23	5	Caution
Donald	ᛞᛟᚾᚨᛚᛞ	147321	18	9	Accomplishment
Douglas	ᛞᛟᚢᚷᛚᚨᛊ	14762310	24	6	Abundance
Drew	ᛞᚱᛖᚹ	1941	15	6	Abundance
Dudley	ᛞᚢᛞᛚᛖᛇ	1712480	23	5	Caution
Duke	ᛞᚢᚲᛖ	17340	15	6	Abundance
Dustin	ᛞᚢᛊᛏᛁᚾ	1713370	22	4	Stability
Eamon	ᛖᚨᛗᛟᚾ	43247	20	2	Friendship
Earl	ᛖᚨᚱᛚ	4392	18	9	Accomplishment
Eddie	ᛖᛞᛞᛁᛖ	41134	13	4	Stability
Edgar	ᛖᛞᚷᚨᚱ	41639	23	5	Caution
Edmund	ᛖᛞᛗᚢᚾᛞ	412771	22	4	Stability
Edwin	ᛖᛞᚹᛁᚾ	41137	16	7	Courage
Elliot	ᛖᛚᛚᛁᛟᛏ	422343	18	9	Accomplishment
Elton	ᛖᛚᛏᛟᚾ	42347	20	2	Friendship
Elvis	ᛖᛚᚹᛁᛊ	42131	11	2	Friendship
Emile	ᛖᛗᛁᛚᛖ	42324	15	6	Abundance
Enrico	ᛖᚾᚱᛁᚲᛟ	479334	30	3	Fertility
Eric	ᛖᚱᛁᚲ	49330	19	1	Victory
Ernest	ᛖᚱᚾᛖᛊᛏ	4974130	28	1	Victory

Name and Numerology

Boy's name	Rune symbols	Rune numbers	Total	Key number	Key word
Ethan	ᛗᛏᚾᛟᚻ	43037	17	8	Dedication
Euan	ᛗᚾᚻ	4737	21	3	Fertility
Eugene	ᛗᚾᛪᛗᛁᛗ	476474	32	5	Caution
Farquhar	ᚠᚱᚱᛟᚾᚾᚱ	639670390	43	7	Courage
Felix	ᚠᛗᚾᛈ	64235	20	2	Friendship
Fenton	ᚠᛗᛁᛏᛟᛁ	6473470	31	4	Stability
Ferdinand	ᚠᛗᚱᛞᛁᚻᚻᛁᛞ	6491373710	41	5	Caution
Fergal	ᚠᛗᚱᛪᚾ	6496320	30	3	Fertility
Fergie	ᚠᛗᚱᛪᛁᛗ	6496340	32	5	Caution
Fernando	ᚠᛗᚱᛁᚻᛞᛞᛩ	64973714	41	5	Caution
Findlay	ᚠᛁᛞᛩᚾᚾ	63712380	30	3	Fertility
Fingal	ᚠᛁᚻᛪᚾ	6376320	27	9	Accomplishment
Finlay	ᚠᛁᚻᚾᚾ	637238	29	2	Friendship
Fitzgerald	ᚠᛁᛏᛃᛪᛗᚱᚾᚻᛞ	63346493210	41	5	Caution
Fitzpatrick	ᚠᛁᛏᛃᛂᛗᛏᚱᛕᚲ	633423393330	42	6	Abundance
Fitzroy	ᚠᛁᛏᛃᚱᛩᚾ	63349480	37	1	Victory
Fleming	ᚠᛁᛗᛈᛁᚻᛪ	62423760	30	3	Fertility
Fletcher	ᚠᛁᛗᛏᛂᚲᚾᛗᚱ	62433049	31	4	Stability
Floyd	ᚠᛏᛩᚾᛞ	624810	21	3	Fertility
Flynn	ᚠᛩᚾᛁᛁ	62877	30	3	Fertility
Forbes	ᚠᛩᚱᛒᛗᛋ	649341	27	9	Accomplishment
Foster	ᚠᛩᛋᛏᛗᚱ	641349	27	9	Accomplishment
Francis	ᚠᚱᚾᛁᚲᛋ	69373310	32	5	Caution
Frank	ᚠᚱᚻᚲ	69373	28	1	Victory
Fraser	ᚠᚱᛋᛗᚱ	693149	32	5	Caution
Frederick	ᚠᚱᛗᛞᛪᛗᚱᚲᚲ	694149333	42	6	Abundance

Book of Runes

Boy's name	Rune symbols	Rune numbers	Total	Key number	Key word
Fritz	ᚠᚱᛁᛏᛦ	69334	25	7	Courage
Fulton	ᚠᚢᛏᛉᚾ	672347	29	2	Friendship
Fyfe	ᚠᛃᛃᛘ	6864	24	6	Abundance
G_Nther	ᚷ ᛃᛏᚾᛘᚱ	60730490	29	2	Friendship
Gabriel	ᚷᚨᛒᚱᛁᛘᛏ	63393420	30	3	Fertility
Gallagher	ᚷᚨᛏᛃᚷᚾᛘᚱ	6322360490	35	8	Dedication
Gareth	ᚷᚨᚱᛘᛏᚾ	639430	25	7	Courage
Garfield	ᚷᚨᚱᚠᛁᛏᛏᛉ	639634210	34	7	Courage
Gary	ᚷᚨᚱᛃ	63980	26	8	Dedication
Gavin	ᚷᚨᛃᛁᚾ	63137	20	2	Friendship
Gawain	ᚷᚨᛃᚾᛁ	631337	23	5	Caution
Gaylord	ᚷᛃᛃᛏᛉᚱᛉ	63824910	33	6	Abundance
Geoffrey	ᚷᛘᛉᚠᚠᚱᛘᛃ	644669480	47	2	Friendship
George	ᚷᛘᛉᚱᚷᛘ	6449640	33	6	Abundance
Geraint	ᚷᛘᚱᚾᛁᛏ	6493373	35	8	Dedication
Gerald	ᚷᛘᚱᚾᛉ	649321	25	7	Courage
Gervais	ᚷᛘᚱᛈᚾᛊ	6491331	27	9	Accomplishment
Gibson	ᚷᛁᛒᛊᛉᚾ	6331470	24	6	Abundance
Gilbert	ᚷᛁᛒᛘᚱᛏ	63234930	30	3	Fertility
Gilchrist	ᚷᛁᛈᚲᚾᚱᛁᛊᛏ	632309313	30	3	Fertility
Gillespie	ᚷᛁᛈᛈᛋᛖᛁᛘ	6322412340	27	9	Accomplishment
Gillies	ᚷᛁᛈᛈᛘᛊ	6322341	21	3	Fertility
Glen	ᚷᛚᛘᛁ	62470	19	1	Victory
Gordon	ᚷᛉᚱᛉᛉᚾ	649147	31	4	Stability
Graham	ᚷᚱᚾᚾᛈᛈ	693032	23	5	Caution
Granger	ᚷᚱᚾᛁᚷᛘᚱ	6937649	44	8	Dedication

Name and Numerology

Boy's name	Rune symbols	Rune numbers	Total	Key number	Key word
Gregor	ᚷᚱᛗᚷᛟᚱ	694649	38	2	Friendship
Guido	ᚷᚢᛁᛞᛟ	67314	21	3	Fertility
Gus	ᚷᚢᛋ	671	14	5	Caution
Guy	ᚷᚢᛁ	678	21	3	Fertility
Hadrian	ᚺᚪᛞᚱᛁᚪᚾ	03193370	26	8	Dedication
Hall	ᚺᚪᛚᛚ	0322	7	7	Courage
Hamish	ᚺᚪᛗᛁᛋᚾ	032310	9	9	Accomplishment
Hank	ᚺᚪᚾᚲ	03730	13	4	Stability
Harold	ᚺᚪᚱᛟᛚᛞ	039421	19	1	Victory
Harris	ᚺᚪᚱᚱᛁᛋ	039931	25	7	Courage
Harry	ᚺᚪᚱᚱᛁ	03998	29	2	Friendship
Hayden	ᚺᚪᛁᛞᛗᚾ	038147	23	5	Caution
Heathcliff	ᚺᛗᚪᛏᚺᚲᛚᛁᚠᚠ	0433032366	30	3	Fertility
Hector	ᚺᛗᚲᛏᛟᚱ	0433490	23	5	Caution
Henry	ᚺᛗᚺᚱᛁ	04798	28	1	Victory
Horace	ᚺᛟᚱᚪᚲᛗ	049334	23	5	Caution
Howard	ᚺᛟᚠᚪᚱᛞ	041391	18	9	Accomplishment
Hubert	ᚺᚢᛒᛗᚱᛏ	0734930	26	8	Dedication
Humphrey	ᚺᚢᛗᛈᚺᚱᛗᛁ	07220948	32	5	Caution
Iain	ᛁᚪᚾ	33370	16	7	Courage
Ike	ᚲᛗ	334	10	1	Victory
Innes	ᛁᚾᚾᛗᛋ	37741	22	4	Stability
Irvine	ᛁᚱᚠᛁᛗ	391374	27	9	Accomplishment
Irwin	ᛁᚱᚠᛁ	39137	23	5	Caution
Isaac	ᛁᛋᚪᚪᚲ	313330	13	4	Stability
Ivan	ᛁᚠᚪ	3137	14	5	Caution

Book of Runes

Boy's name	Rune symbols	Rune numbers	Total	Key number	Key word
Ivor	ᛁᚦᛩᚱ	3149	17	8	Dedication
Izaak	ᛁᛉᛘᚲ	34333	16	7	Courage
Jack	ᛋᚲᚲᚲ	83330	17	8	Dedication
Jacob	ᛋᚲᚲᛩᛒ	83343	21	3	Fertility
Jaime	ᛋᚼᛈᛠ	83324	20	2	Friendship
Jake	ᛋᚲᚲᛠ	83340	18	9	Accomplishment
Jarvis	ᛋᚼᚱᛈᛁᛋ	839131	25	7	Courage
Jason	ᛋᚲᛋᛩᚻ	83147	23	5	Caution
Jedidiah	ᛋᛗᛞᚫᛞᚫᛁᚼ	841313300	23	5	Caution
Jefferson	ᛋᛗᚠᚠᛗᚱᛋᛩᚻ	846649147	49	4	Stability
Jeffrey	ᛋᛗᚠᚠᚱᛗᛁ	8466948	45	9	Accomplishment
Jeremy	ᛋᛗᚱᛗᛈᛁ	849428	35	8	Dedication
Jerry	ᛋᛗᚱᚱᛁ	84998	38	2	Friendship
Jesse	ᛋᛗᛋᛋᛗ	841140	18	9	Accomplishment
Jethro	ᛋᛗᛏᚾᚱᛩ	843094	28	1	Victory
Jim	ᛋᛁᛈ	832	13	4	Stability
Jock	ᛋᛩᚲᚲ	8433	18	9	Accomplishment
Joe	ᛋᛩᛠ	844	16	7	Courage
John	ᛋᛩᚻᚻ	84070	19	1	Victory
Jonathon	ᛋᛩᚻᛈᛏᚾᛩᚻ	84733047	36	9	Accomplishment
Jordan	ᛋᛩᚱᛞᚫᚻ	849137	32	5	Caution
Joseph	ᛋᛩᛋᛗᛈᚾ	8414200	19	1	Victory
Jude	ᛋᚾᛞᛠ	8714	20	2	Friendship
Julian	ᛋᚾᚾᚻ	872337	30	3	Fertility
Julius	ᛋᚾᚾᚾᛋ	872371	28	1	Victory
Justin	ᛋᚾᛋᛏᚻ	8713370	29	2	Friendship

Boy's name	Rune symbols	Rune numbers	Total	Key number	Key word
Kane	ᚲᚨᚾᛗ	3374	17	8	Dedication
Karl	ᚲᚨᚱᛚ	33920	17	8	Dedication
Keegan	ᚲᛗᛗᚷᚨᚾ	344637	27	9	Accomplishment
Keir	ᚲᛗᛁᚱ	34390	19	1	Victory
Keith	ᚲᛗᛁᛏᚾ	343300	13	4	Stability
Ken	ᚲᛗᚾ	3470	14	5	Caution
Kendall	ᚲᛗᚾᛞᚨᛚᛚ	3471322	22	4	Stability
Kennedy	ᚲᛗᚾᚾᛗᛞᚲᛃ	3477418	34	7	Courage
Kenneth	ᚲᛗᚾᚾᛗᛏᚾ	3477430	28	1	Victory
Kerr	ᚲᛗᚱᚱ	34990	25	7	Courage
Kevin	ᚲᛗᚹᛁᚾ	34137	18	9	Accomplishment
Kieran	ᚲᛁᛗᚱᚨᚾ	3349370	29	2	Friendship
Kirk	ᚲᛁᚱᚲ	33930	18	9	Accomplishment
Kris	ᚲᚱᛁᛋ	39310	16	7	Courage
Kristen	ᚲᚱᛁᛋᛏᛗᚾ	3931347	30	3	Fertility
Kurt	ᚲᚢᚱᛏ	37930	22	4	Stability
Kyle	ᚲᛃᛚᛗ	3824	17	8	Dedication
Lachlan	ᛚᚨᚲᚺᛚᚨᚾ	23302370	20	2	Friendship
Lance	ᛚᚨᚾᚲᛗ	237340	19	1	Victory
Lancelot	ᛚᚨᚾᚲᛗᛚᛟᛏ	237342430	28	1	Victory
Larry	ᛚᚨᚱᚱᛃ	239980	31	4	Stability
Laurence	ᛚᚨᚢᚱᛗᚾᚲᛗ	23794734	39	3	Fertility
Laurie	ᛚᚨᚢᚱᛁᛗ	2379340	28	1	Victory
Lawrence	ᛚᚨᚹᚱᛗᚾᚲᛗ	23194734	33	6	Abundance
Lawson	ᛚᚨᚹᛋᛟᚾ	231147	18	9	Accomplishment
Lee	ᛚᛗᛗ	244	10	1	Victory

Boy's name	Rune symbols	Rune numbers	Total	Key number	Key word
Leif	ᛖᛁᛁᚹ	24360	15	6	Abundance
Lenny	ᛖᛁᚺᚺᛋ	247780	28	1	Victory
Leo	ᛖᛁᛉ	2440	10	1	Victory
Leon	ᛖᛁᛉᚺ	2447	17	8	Dedication
Leonardo	ᛖᛁᛉᚺᚱᚱᛇᛉ	244739140	34	7	Courage
Leroy	ᛖᛁᚱᛉᛋ	249480	27	9	Accomplishment
Leslie	ᛖᛁᛋᛁᛁ	2412340	16	7	Courage
Lester	ᛖᛁᛋᛏᛁᚱ	2413490	23	5	Caution
Levi	ᛖᛁᚹᛁ	24130	10	1	Victory
Lewis	ᛖᛁᚹᛁᛋ	241310	11	2	Friendship
Liam	ᛁᚱᛗ	23320	10	1	Victory
Lincoln	ᛁᚺᚲᛉᚺ	23734270	28	1	Victory
Lindsay	ᛁᚺᛇᛋᚱᛋ	2371138	25	7	Courage
Lionel	ᛁᛉᚺᛗ	2347420	22	4	Stability
Llewelyn	ᛁᛁᚹᛗᛁᛋᚺ	22414287	30	3	Fertility
Lloyd	ᛁᛉᛋᛇ	224810	17	8	Dedication
Logan	ᛚᛉᚷᚺ	246370	22	4	Stability
Lonnie	ᛚᛉᚺᚺᛗ	2477340	27	9	Accomplishment
Lorne	ᛚᛉᚱᚺᛗ	249740	26	8	Dedication
Lou	ᛚᛉᚢ	247	13	4	Stability
Louis	ᛚᛉᚢᛁᛋ	247310	17	8	Dedication
Lucan	ᛗᚲᚱᚺ	273370	22	4	Stability
Lucas	ᛗᚲᚱᛋ	27331	16	7	Courage
Luke	ᛗᚲᛗ	2734	16	7	Courage
Lyle	ᛋᛗᛗ	2824	16	7	Courage
Lytton	ᛋᛏᛏᛉᚺ	283347	27	9	Accomplishment

Boy's name	Rune symbols	Rune numbers	Total	Key number	Key word
Magnus		2367710	26	8	Dedication
Malachi		23233030	16	7	Courage
Malcolm		2323422	18	9	Accomplishment
Mallory		2322498	30	3	Fertility
Manfred		2376941	32	5	Caution
Manuel		237742	25	7	Courage
Marco		239340	21	3	Fertility
Mario		23934	21	3	Fertility
Mark		2393	17	8	Dedication
Marlow		2392410	21	3	Fertility
Marshall		239103220	22	4	Stability
Martin		239337	27	9	Accomplishment
Marty		23938	25	7	Courage
Marvin		239137	25	7	Courage
Matthew		2333041	16	7	Courage
Maurice		23793340	31	4	Stability
Maximilian		23532323370	33	6	Abundance
Maxwell		23514220	19	1	Victory
Maynard		23873910	33	6	Abundance
Merlin		249237	27	9	Accomplishment
Michael		2330342	17	8	Dedication
Mick		2333	11	2	Friendship
Mikael		233342	17	8	Dedication
Miles		232410	12	3	Fertility
Miller		2322490	22	4	Stability
Milne		232740	18	9	Accomplishment

Boy's name	Rune symbols	Rune numbers	Total	Key number	Key word
Mitchell	ᛗᛁᛏᚲᚺᛖᛚᛚ	233304220	19	1	Victory
Montague	ᛗᛟᚾᛏᚨᚷᚢᛖ	24733674	36	9	Accomplishment
Montgomery	ᛗᛟᚾᛏᚷᛟᛗᛖᚱᛃ	2473642498	49	4	Stability
Monty	ᛗᛟᚾᛏᛃ	247380	24	6	Abundance
Mortimer	ᛗᛟᚱᛏᛁᛗᛖᚱ	24933249	36	9	Accomplishment
Morton	ᛗᛟᚱᛏᛟᚾ	2493470	29	2	Friendship
Mungo	ᛗᚢᚾᚷᛟ	277640	26	8	Dedication
Murdo	ᛗᚢᚱᛞᛟ	27914	23	5	Caution
Murray	ᛗᚢᚱᚱᛃ	2799380	38	2	Friendship
Myles	ᛗᛃᛚᛖᛋ	28241	17	8	Dedication
Nairn	ᚾᚨᛁᚱᚾ	73397	29	2	Friendship
Napier	ᚾᚨᛈᛁᛖᚱ	7323490	28	1	Victory
Nash	ᚾᚨᛋᚺ	7310	11	2	Friendship
Nathan	ᚾᚨᛏᚺᚨᚾ	733037	23	5	Caution
Ned	ᚾᛖᛞ	741	12	3	Fertility
Neil	ᚾᛖᛁᛚ	74320	16	7	Courage
Nelson	ᚾᛖᛚᛋᛟᚾ	7421470	25	7	Courage
Nero	ᚾᛖᚱᛟ	74940	24	6	Abundance
Nicholas	ᚾᛁᚲᚺᛟᛚᚨᛋ	73304231	23	5	Caution
Nick	ᚾᛁᚲᚲ	73330	16	7	Courage
Nigel	ᚾᛁᚷᛖᛚ	736420	22	4	Stability
Ninian	ᚾᛁᚾᛁᚨᚾ	737337	30	3	Fertility
Nixon	ᚾᛁᛒᛟᚾ	735470	26	8	Dedication
Nolan	ᚾᛟᛚᚨᚾ	742370	23	5	Caution
Norman	ᚾᛟᚱᛗᚨᚾ	749237	32	5	Caution
Norton	ᚾᛟᚱᛏᛟᚾ	7493470	34	7	Courage

Boy's name	*Rune symbols*	*Rune numbers*	*Total*	*Key number*	*Key word*
Obadiah	ᛟᛒᚨᛞᛁᚨᚺ	43313300	17	8	Dedication
Oberon	ᛟᛒᛖᚱᛟᚾ	434947	31	4	Stability
Ogilvie	ᛟᚷᛁᛚᚹᛁᛖ	4632134	23	5	Caution
Oliver	ᛟᛚᛁᚹᛖᚱ	423149	23	5	Caution
Omar	ᛟᛗᚨᚱ	4239	18	9	Accomplishment
Orion	ᛟᚱᛁᛟᚾ	493470	27	9	Accomplishment
Orlando	ᛟᚱᛚᚨᚾᛞᛟ	49237140	30	3	Fertility
Orpheus	ᛟᚱᛈᚺᛖᚢᛊ	4920471	27	9	Accomplishment
Orson	ᛟᚱᛊᛟᚾ	491470	25	7	Courage
Osborn	ᛟᛊᛒᛟᚱᚾ	413497	28	1	Victory
Oscar	ᛟᛊᚲᚨᚱ	41339	20	2	Friendship
Osmond	ᛟᛊᛗᛟᚾᛞ	412471	19	1	Victory
Oswald	ᛟᛊᚹᚨᛚᛞ	411321	12	3	Fertility
Otis	ᛟᛏᛁᛊ	43310	11	2	Friendship
Otto	ᛟᛏᛏᛟ	43340	14	5	Caution
Owen	ᛟᚹᛖᚾ	41470	16	7	Courage
Oxford	ᛟᚦᚠᛟᚱᛞ	456491	29	2	Friendship
Pablo	ᛈᚨᛒᛚᛟ	233240	14	5	Caution
Paddy	ᛈᚨᛞᛞᛇ	23118	15	6	Abundance
Padraig	ᛈᚨᛞᚱᚨᛁᚷ	23193360	27	9	Accomplishment
Paolo	ᛈᚨᛟᛚᛟ	234240	15	6	Abundance
Pascal	ᛈᚨᛊᚲᚨᛚ	231332	14	5	Caution
Pat	ᛈᚨᛏ	2330	8	8	Dedication
Patrick	ᛈᚨᛏᚱᛁᚲᚲ	23393330	26	8	Dedication
Paul	ᛈᚨᚢᛚ	2372	14	5	Caution
Pedro	ᛈᛖᛞᚱᛟ	241940	20	2	Friendship

Boy's name	Rune symbols	Rune numbers	Total	Key number	Key word
Pepe	ᚲᛗᚲᛗ	2424	12	3	Fertility
Percival	ᚲᛗᚱᚲᛈᚾ	24933132	27	9	Accomplishment
Percy	ᚲᛗᚱᚲᛃ	24938	26	8	Dedication
Peregrine	ᚲᛗᚱᛗᚷᚱᚺᛗ	2494693740	48	3	Fertility
Peter	ᚲᛗᛏᛗᚱ	243490	22	4	Stability
Phil	ᚲᚾᛁ	20320	7	7	Courage
Philip	ᚲᚾᛁᚾᚲ	2032320	12	3	Fertility
Pierce	ᚲᛁᛗᚱᚲᛗ	2349340	25	7	Courage
Pierre	ᚲᛁᛗᚱᚱᛗ	2349940	31	4	Stability
Placido	ᚲᛁᚠᚲᛞᚷ	2233314	18	9	Accomplishment
Plato	ᚲᛁᚠᛏᚷ	223340	14	5	Caution
Pr_Spero	ᚲᚱ ᛋᛗᛗᚱᚷ	290124940	31	4	Stability
Presley	ᚲᚱᛗᛋᛏᛗᛃ	2941248	30	3	Fertility
Rab	ᚱᚨᛒ	933	15	6	Abundance
Radcliffe	ᚱᚨᛞᚲᚾᛈᛈᛗ	9313236640	37	1	Victory
Raffaele	ᚱᚨᛈᛈᚾᛗᛗ	93663424	37	1	Victory
Rafferty	ᚱᚨᛈᛈᛗᚱᛏᛃ	93664938	48	3	Fertility
Ralph	ᚱᚨᛏᚲᚾ	932200	16	7	Courage
Ramsay	ᚱᚨᛗᛋᚱᛃ	932138	26	8	Dedication
Ramsden	ᚱᚨᛗᛋᛞᚷᛗᚺ	9321147	27	9	Accomplishment
Randal	ᚱᚨᚺᛞᚨᚾ	937132	25	7	Courage
Randolf	ᚱᚨᚺᛞᚷᚱᛈ	9371426	32	5	Caution
Rankin	ᚱᚨᚲᚺ	937337	32	5	Caution
Raoul	ᚱᚨᚷᛏ	934720	25	7	Courage
Raphael	ᚱᚨᚲᚾᚨᛏ	93203420	23	5	Caution
Rastus	ᚱᚨᛋᛏᛃᛋ	9313710	24	6	Abundance

Boy's name	Rune symbols	Rune numbers	Total	Key number	Key word
Ray	ᚱᚨᛁ	938	20	2	Friendship
Raymond	ᚱᚨᛁᛗᛟᚾᛞ	9382471	34	7	Courage
Reagan	ᚱᛖᚨᚷᚨᚾ	9436370	32	5	Caution
Redmond	ᚱᛖᛞᛗᛟᚾᛞ	9412471	28	1	Victory
Reece	ᚱᛖᛖᚲᛖ	944340	24	6	Abundance
Reed	ᚱᛖᛖᛞ	9441	18	9	Accomplishment
Reeve	ᚱᛖᛖᚹᛖ	94414	22	4	Stability
Regan	ᚱᛖᚷᚨᚾ	946370	29	2	Friendship
Reginald	ᚱᛖᚷᛁᚾᚨᛚᛞ	94637321	35	8	Dedication
Reilly	ᚱᛖᛁᛚᛚᛁ	9432280	28	1	Victory
Reinhold	ᚱᛖᛁᚾᚺᛟᛚᛞ	943704210	30	3	Fertility
Renaldo	ᚱᛖᚾᚨᛚᛞᛟ	9473214	30	3	Fertility
Renfrew	ᚱᛖᚾᚠᚱᛖᚹ	9476941	40	4	Stability
Rennie	ᚱᛖᚾᚾᛁᛖ	947734	34	7	Courage
Renton	ᚱᛖᚾᛏᛟᚾ	9473470	34	7	Courage
Rex	ᚱᛖᚹ	9450	18	9	Accomplishment
Reynard	ᚱᛖᛁᚾᚨᚱᛞ	94873910	41	5	Caution
Rhodri	ᚱᚺᛟᛞᚱᛁ	9041930	26	8	Dedication
Ricardo	ᚱᛁᚲᚨᚱᛞᛟ	93339140	32	5	Caution
Richard	ᚱᛁᚲᚺᚨᚱᛞ	9330391	28	1	Victory
Richmond	ᚱᛁᚲᚺᛗᛟᚾᛞ	933024710	29	2	Friendship
Ridley	ᚱᛁᛞᛚᛖᛁ	931248	27	9	Accomplishment
Rigby	ᚱᛁᚷᛒᛁ	936380	29	2	Friendship
Riley	ᚱᛁᛚᛖᛁ	932480	26	8	Dedication
Riordan	ᚱᛁᛟᚱᛞᚨᚾ	93491370	36	9	Accomplishment
Ripley	ᚱᛁᛈᛚᛖᛁ	932248	28	1	Victory

Book of Runes

Boy's name	Rune symbols	Rune numbers	Total	Key number	Key word
Ritchie	ᚱᛁᛏᚲᚾᛁᛖ	93330340	25	7	Courage
Roald	ᚱᚩᚪᛚᛞ	94321	19	1	Victory
Robert	ᚱᚩᛒᛖᚱᛏ	9434930	32	5	Caution
Robyn	ᚱᚩᛒᚾ	943870	31	4	Stability
Rochester	ᚱᚩᚲᚾᛗᛋᛏᛖᚱ	943041349	37	1	Victory
Rocky	ᚱᚩᚲᚲᛋ	943380	27	9	Accomplishment
Rodden	ᚱᚩᛞᛞᛖᛗ	941147	26	8	Dedication
Roddy	ᚱᚩᛞᛞᛚᛋ	94118	23	5	Caution
Roderick	ᚱᚩᛞᛖᚱᚲᚲ	94149333	36	9	Accomplishment
Rodger	ᚱᚩᛞᛖᚷᛖᚱ	941649	33	6	Abundance
Rodrigo	ᚱᚩᛞᚱᛁᚷᚩ	9419364	36	9	Accomplishment
Roger	ᚱᚩᚷᛖᚱ	946490	32	5	Caution
Roland	ᚱᚩᛚᚾᛞ	942371	26	8	Dedication
Rolf	ᚱᚩᛚᚠ	94260	21	3	Fertility
Romeo	ᚱᚩᛗᛖᛗᚩ	94244	23	5	Caution
Ronald	ᚱᚩᚻᚾᛞ	9473210	26	8	Dedication
Rooney	ᚱᚩᚩᚻᛗᛋ	9447480	36	9	Accomplishment
Rory	ᚱᚩᚱᛋ	94980	30	3	Fertility
Roslin	ᚱᚩᛋᚾᛁ	941237	26	8	Dedication
Ross	ᚱᚩᛋᛋ	94110	15	6	Abundance
Rowan	ᚱᚩᛈᚾ	94137	24	6	Abundance
Roy	ᚱᚩᛋ	9480	21	3	Fertility
Royston	ᚱᚩᛋᛏᚩᛁ	9481347	36	9	Accomplishment
Ruben	ᚱᚢᛒᛖᛁ	97347	30	3	Fertility
Rudi	ᚱᚢᛞᛁ	97130	20	2	Friendship
Rudolph	ᚱᚢᛞᚩᚱᚢᚻ	9714220	25	7	Courage

Boy's name	Rune symbols	Rune numbers	Total	Key number	Key word
Rudyard	ᚱᚾᛞᛃᛢᚨᚱᛞ	9718391	38	2	Friendship
Russell	ᚱᚾᛋᛋᛗᛏᛏ	9711422	26	8	Dedication
Rutger	ᚱᚾᛏᚷᛗᚱ	9736490	38	2	Friendship
Ryan	ᚱᛃᛂᛏ	98370	27	9	Accomplishment
Salvador	ᛋᛂᛏᛒᛞᛢᚨᚱ	13213149	24	6	Abundance
Sam	ᛋᛂᛗ	1320	6	6	Abundance
Samuel	ᛋᛒᛂᛏᛏ	132742	19	1	Victory
Sandy	ᛋᛂᛂᛞᛃ	137180	20	2	Friendship
Saxon	ᛋᛂᚦᚨᛏ	13547	20	2	Friendship
Scott	ᛋᚲᚨᛏᛏ	134330	14	5	Caution
Sean	ᛋᛏᛂᛏ	14370	15	6	Abundance
Sebastian	ᛋᛖᛒᛂᛋᛏᛂᛏ	1433133370	28	1	Victory
Selby	ᛋᛖᛏᛒᛃ	142380	18	9	Accomplishment
Selden	ᛋᛖᛏᛞᛖᛏ	142147	19	1	Victory
Sergio	ᛋᛖᚱᚷᛁᚨ	1496340	27	9	Accomplishment
Seth	ᛋᛖᛏᚼ	1430	8	8	Dedication
Seton	ᛋᛖᛏᚨᛏ	14347	19	1	Victory
Seumas	ᛋᛖᛏᛒᛁᛋ	147231	18	9	Accomplishment
Shamus	ᛋᚾᛂᛗᛃᛋ	103271	14	5	Caution
Shane	ᛋᚾᛂᛃᛗ	10374	15	6	Abundance
Sheldon	ᛋᚾᛖᛏᛞᚨᛢᛏ	1042147	19	1	Victory
Sheridan	ᛋᚾᛖᚱᛁᛞᛂᛏ	10493137	28	1	Victory
Sherman	ᛋᚾᛖᚱᛗᛂᛏ	1049237	26	8	Dedication
Sidney	ᛋᛁᛞᛃᛗᛃ	131748	24	6	Abundance
Siegfried	ᛋᛁᛗᚷᚠᚱᛁᛗᛞ	134669341	37	1	Victory
Silvano	ᛋᛁᛂᚨᛏᚨ	1321374	21	3	Fertility

Boy's name	*Rune symbols*	*Rune numbers*	*Total*	*Key number*	*Key word*
Silvester	ᛊᛁᛚᚹᛖᛊᛏᛖᚱ	132141349	28	1	Victory
Simon	ᛊᛁᛗᛟᚾ	13247	17	8	Dedication
Sinclair	ᛊᛁᚾᚲᛚᚨᛁᚱ	13732339	31	4	Stability
Smith	ᛊᛗᛁᛏᚺ	12330	9	9	Accomplishment
Sol	ᛊᛟᛚ	142	7	7	Courage
Solomon	ᛊᛟᛚᛟᛗᛟᚾ	1424247	24	6	Abundance
Somerset	ᛊᛟᛗᛖᚱᛊᛖᛏ	14249143	28	1	Victory
Spencer	ᛊᛈᛖᚾᚲᛖᚱ	1247349	30	3	Fertility
Stephen	ᛊᛏᛖᛈᚺᛖᚾ	1342047	21	3	Fertility
Stewart	ᛊᛏᛖᚹᚨᚱᛏ	134139300	24	6	Abundance
Stirling	ᛊᛏᛁᚱᛚᛁᚾᚷ	1339237600	34	7	Courage
Strachan	ᛊᛏᚱᚨᚲᚺᚨᚾ	13933037	29	2	Friendship
Stuart	ᛊᛏᚢᚨᚱᛏ	137393	26	8	Dedication
Sydney	ᛊᛇᛞᚾᛖᛇ	1817480	29	2	Friendship
Sylvester	ᛊᛇᛚᚹᛖᛊᛏᛖᚱ	18214134900	33	6	Abundance
Taffy	ᛏᚨᚠᚠᛇ	3366800	26	8	Dedication
Taggart	ᛏᚨᚷᚷᚨᚱᛏ	33663930	33	6	Abundance
Talbot	ᛏᚨᛚᛒᛟᛏ	33234300	18	9	Accomplishment
Tam	ᛏᚨᛗ	33200	8	8	Dedication
Tate	ᛏᚨᛏᛖ	33340	13	4	Stability
Taylor	ᛏᚨᛇᛚᛟᚱ	33824900	29	2	Friendship
Ted	ᛏᛖᛞ	341	8	8	Dedication
Terence	ᛏᛖᚱᛖᚾᚲᛖ	349473400	34	7	Courage
Theo	ᛏᚺᛖᛟ	30440	11	2	Friendship
Theodore	ᛏᚺᛖᛟᛞᛟᚱᛖ	304414940	29	2	Friendship
Theron	ᛏᚺᛖᚱᛟᚾ	3049470	27	9	Accomplishment

Boy's name	*Rune symbols*	*Rune numbers*	*Total*	*Key number*	*Key word*
Thomas	ᛏᚺᛟᛗᚨᛊ	30423100	13	4	Stability
Thor	ᛏᚺᛟᚱ	30490	16	7	Courage
Thorp	ᛏᚺᛟᚱᛈ	30492	18	9	Accomplishment
Thurstan	ᛏᚺᚢᚱᛊᛏᚨᚾ	30791337	33	6	Abundance
Tibold	ᛏᛁᛒᛟᛚᛞ	3334210	16	7	Courage
Tiernan	ᛏᛁᛖᚱᚾᚨᚾ	3349737	36	9	Accomplishment
Tim	ᛏᛁᛗ	33200	8	8	Dedication
Timothy	ᛏᛁᛗᛟᛏᚺᛇ	332430800	23	5	Caution
Titian	ᛏᛁᛏᛁᚨᚾ	33333700	22	4	Stability
Tobias	ᛏᛟᛒᛁᚨᛊ	343331	17	8	Dedication
Todd	ᛏᛟᛞᛞ	34110	9	9	Accomplishment
Tony	ᛏᛟᚾᛇ	34780	22	4	Stability
Torquil	ᛏᛟᚱᛜᚢᛁᛚ	349673200	34	7	Courage
Travis	ᛏᚱᚨᚹᛁᛊ	3931310	20	2	Friendship
Trevor	ᛏᚱᛖᚹᛟᚱ	39414900	30	3	Fertility
Tristan	ᛏᚱᛁᛊᛏᚨᚾ	39313370	29	2	Friendship
Troy	ᛏᚱᛟᛇ	39480	24	6	Abundance
Trueman	ᛏᚱᚢᛖᛗᚨᚾ	3974237	35	8	Dedication
Tudor	ᛏᚢᛞᛟᚱ	371490	24	6	Abundance
Tully	ᛏᚢᛚᛚᛇ	372280	22	4	Stability
Turner	ᛏᚢᚱᚾᛖᚱ	3797490	39	3	Fertility
Tyler	ᛏᛇᛚᛖᚱ	382490	26	8	Dedication
Tyrone	ᛏᛇᚱᛟᚾᛖ	3894740	35	8	Dedication
Tyson	ᛏᛇᛊᛟᚾ	381470	23	5	Caution
Uberto	ᚢᛒᛖᚱᛏᛟ	7349340	30	3	Fertility
Ulric	ᚢᛚᚱᛁᚲ	72933	24	6	Abundance

Book of Runes

Boy's name	Rune symbols	Rune numbers	Total	Key number	Key word
Ulysses	ᚾᚾᛋᛋᛗᛋ	72811410	24	6	Abundance
Umberto	ᚾᛗᛒᛗᚱᛏᛟ	72349340	32	5	Caution
Uri	ᚾᚱᛁ	7930	19	1	Victory
Uriel	ᚾᚱᛁᛗᛏ	793420	25	7	Courage
Valentino	ᛈᚾᛗᛁᛏᛁᚼᛟ	1324733740	34	7	Courage
Valerian	ᛈᚾᛗᚱᛁᚾᚼ	132493370	32	5	Caution
Vance	ᛈᚼᚲᛗ	13734	18	9	Accomplishment
Vaughan	ᛈᚾᚷᚾᚼᚼ	1376037	27	9	Accomplishment
Vernon	ᛈᛗᚱᛁᛟᚼ	1497470	32	5	Caution
Victor	ᛈᚲᛏᛟᚱ	133349	23	5	Caution
Vidal	ᛈᛁᛞᚾᚾ	131320	10	1	Victory
Vincent	ᛈᚼᚲᛗᚼᛏ	1373473	28	1	Victory
Vinnie	ᛈᚼᚾᛁᛗ	137734	25	7	Courage
Virgil	ᛈᚱᚷᚾᛁ	1396320	24	6	Abundance
Vittorio	ᛈᛁᛏᛏᛟᚱᛁᛟ	133349340	30	3	Fertility
Vladimir	ᛈᚾᚾᛞᛁᛗᛁᚱ	123132390	24	6	Abundance
Walker	ᛈᚾᚾᚲᛗᚱ	1323490	22	4	Stability
Wallace	ᛈᚾᚾᚾᚲᛗ	13223340	18	9	Accomplishment
Wallis	ᛈᚾᚾᛁᛋ	132231	12	3	Fertility
Walt	ᛈᚾᚾᛏ	13230	9	9	Accomplishment
Walter	ᛈᚾᛗᛏᛗᚱ	1323490	22	4	Stability
Ward	ᛈᚾᚱᛞ	13910	14	5	Caution
Warne	ᛈᚾᚱᚼᛗ	139740	24	6	Abundance
Warren	ᛈᚾᚱᚱᛗᚼ	1399470	33	6	Abundance
Wayne	ᛈᚾᚾᚼᛗ	138740	23	5	Caution
Webster	ᛈᛗᛒᛋᛏᛗᚱ	14313490	25	7	Courage

Name and Numerology

Boy's name	Rune symbols	Rune numbers	Total	Key number	Key word
Wendel	ᛟᛖᚾᛞᛖᛚ	147142	19	1	Victory
Wilbur	ᚹᛁᛚᛒᚢᚱ	1323790	25	7	Courage
Wilfrid	ᚹᛁᛚᚠᚱᛁᛞ	1326931	25	7	Courage
William	ᚹᛁᛚᛚᛁᛗ	13223320	16	7	Courage
Wilson	ᚹᛁᛚᛊᛟᚾ	1321470	18	9	Accomplishment
Winston	ᚹᛁᚾᛊᛏᛟᚾ	13713470	26	8	Dedication
Wolf	ᚹᛟᛚᚠ	1426	13	4	Stability
Woodrow	ᚹᛟᛟᛞᚱᛟᚹ	14419410	24	6	Abundance
Xavier	ᛉᚨᚹᛁᛖᚱ	5313490	25	7	Courage
Xenos	ᛉᛖᚾᛟᛊ	547410	21	3	Fertility
Yves	ᛃᚹᛖᛊ	81410	14	5	Caution
Zachary	ᛜᚨᚲᚺᚨᚱᛊ	4330398	30	3	Fertility
Zebadiah	ᛜᛖᛒᚨᛞᛁᚨᚺ	44331330	21	3	Fertility
Zeke	ᛜᛖᚲᛖ	44340	15	6	Abundance

Book of Runes

Girl's name	Rune symbols	Rune numbers	Total	Key number	Key word
Abbie	ᚾᛒᛒᛁᛗ	33334	16	7	Courage
Abigail	ᚾᛒᛁ᚜ᚾᛐ	3336332	23	5	Caution
Acacia	ᚱ᚜ᚱ᚜ᛁᚱ	333333	18	9	Accomplishment
Ada	ᚾ᚜ᛁᚱ	313	7	7	Courage
Adina	ᚾ᚜ᛁᚺᛐ	31373	17	8	Dedication
Adora	ᚾ᚜ᛁ᚜ᚱᚱᛐ	31493	20	2	Friendship
Adorna	ᚾ᚜ᛁ᚜ᚱᚱᛁᛐ	314973	27	9	Accomplishment
Adrianne	ᚾ᚜ᚱᛁᛁᛐᚺᛗ	31933774	37	1	Victory
Agnes	ᚱᚷᛁᛐᛗᛋ	36741	21	3	Fertility
Ailean	ᛁᛁᛐᛁᛐ	332437	22	4	Stability
Ailsa	ᛁᛁᛋᚱ	33213	12	3	Fertility
Aimée	ᛁᛁᛁᛗᛗ	33244	16	7	Courage
Aine	ᛁᚺᛗ	3374	17	8	Dedication
Aisleen	ᛁᛋᛁᛐᛗᛁ	3312447	24	6	Abundance
Alys	ᚾᛐᛋ	3281	14	5	Caution
Alyth	ᚾᛐᛐᚺ	32830	16	7	Courage
Amabel	ᛁᛁᛒᛗᛐ	323342	17	8	Dedication
Amalia	ᛁᛁᛐᛁᚱ	323233	16	7	Courage
Amanda	ᛁᛁᛐᚺ᚜ᚱ	323713	19	1	Victory
Anatolia	ᛁᚺᛗᛐᚱᛐᚱ	37334233	28	1	Victory
Andrea	ᛁᚺ᚜ᚱᛗᛁ	371943	27	9	Accomplishment
Andrina	ᛁᚺ᚜ᚱᛁᚺᚱ	3719373	33	6	Abundance
Anemone	ᛁᛗᛁᚹ᚜ᛗ	3742474	31	4	Stability
Angel	ᚺᚷᚱᛐ	37642	22	4	Stability
Angela	ᚺᚷᚱᛐᚱ	376423	25	7	Courage

Name and Numerology

Girl's name	Rune symbols	Rune numbers	Total	Key number	Key word
Angelica	ᚻᚷᚷᛖᚾᚲᚨ	37642333	31	4	Stability
Bab	ᛒᚨᛒ	333	9	9	Accomplishment
Bambi	ᛒᚨᛗᛒᛁ	33233	14	5	Caution
Baptista	ᛒᚨᛈᛏᛁᛋᛏᚨ	33233133	21	3	Fertility
Barbara	ᛒᚨᚱᛒᚨᚱᚨ	3393393	33	6	Abundance
Basilia	ᛒᚨᛋᛁᚾᚨ	3313233	18	9	Accomplishment
Beata	ᛒᛖᚨᛏᚨ	34333	16	7	Courage
Beatrice	ᛒᛖᚨᛏᚱᚲᛖ	34339334	32	5	Caution
Beckie	ᛒᛖᚲᚲᛁᛖ	343334	20	2	Friendship
Beda	ᛒᛖᛞᚨ	3413	11	2	Friendship
Bee	ᛒᛖᛖ	344	11	2	Friendship
Beerthilda	ᛒᛖᛖᚱᛏᚾᛁᛚᛞᚨ	3449303213	32	5	Caution
Benita	ᛒᛖᚾᛁᛏᚨ	347333	23	5	Caution
Berenice	ᛒᛖᚱᛖᚾᚲᛖ	34947334	37	1	Victory
Bernadette	ᛒᛖᚱᚾᚨᛞᛖᛏᛏᛖ	3497314334	41	5	Caution
Bernice	ᛒᛖᚱᚾᚲᛖ	3497334	33	6	Abundance
Berta	ᛒᛖᚱᛏᚨ	34933	22	4	Stability
Berte	ᛒᛖᚱᛏᛖ	34934	23	5	Caution
Beth	ᛒᛖᛏᚾ	3430	10	1	Victory
Bethan	ᛒᛖᛏᚾᚨᚾ	343037	20	2	Friendship
Bethany	ᛒᛖᛏᚾᚨᚾᛋ	3430378	28	1	Victory
Betsy	ᛒᛖᛏᛋᛋ	34318	19	1	Victory
Beulah	ᛒᛖᚢᚾᚨᚾ	347230	19	1	Victory
Bianca	ᛒᛁᚾᚲᚨ	333733	22	4	Stability
Blanca	ᛒᚾᚾᚲᚨ	323733	21	3	Fertility

203

Girl's name	Rune symbols	Rune numbers	Total	Key number	Key word
Blanche	ᛒᛚᚨᚾᚲᚺᛖ	3237304	22	4	Stability
Caddie	ᚲᚨᛞᛞᛁᛖ	331134	15	6	Abundance
Caitlín	ᚲᚨᛁᛏᛚᛁ	3333237	24	6	Abundance
Callista	ᚲᚨᛚᛚᛁᛋᛏᚨ	33223133	20	2	Friendship
Camilla	ᚲᚨᛗᛁᛚᛚᚨ	3323223	18	9	Accomplishment
Candy	ᚲᚨᚾᛞᛃ	33718	22	4	Stability
Carla	ᚲᚨᚱᛚᚨ	33923	20	2	Friendship
Carlin	ᚲᚨᚱᛚᛁ	339237	27	9	Accomplishment
Carolina	ᚲᚨᚱᛟᛚᛁᚾᚨ	33942373	34	7	Courage
Carys	ᚲᚨᚱᛃᛋ	33981	24	6	Abundance
Catherine	ᚲᚨᛏᚺᛖᚱᛁᚾᛖ	333049374	36	9	Accomplishment
Cecile	ᚲᛖᚲᛁᛚᛖ	343324	19	1	Victory
Cecily	ᚲᛖᚲᛁᛚᛃ	343328	23	5	Caution
Celeste	ᚲᛖᛚᛖᛋᛏᛖ	3424134	21	3	Fertility
Cerian	ᚲᛖᚱᛁᚾ	349337	29	2	Friendship
Cheryl	ᚲᚺᛖᚱᛃᛚ	304982	26	8	Dedication
Chloë	ᚲᚺᛚᛟᛖ	30244	13	4	Stability
Chrissie	ᚲᚺᚱᛁᛋᛋᛁᛖ	30931134	24	6	Abundance
Christy	ᚲᚺᚱᛁᛋᛏᛃ	3093138	27	9	Accomplishment
Cicely	ᚲᚲᛖᛏᛃ	333428	23	5	Caution
Cilla	ᚲᛁᛚᛚᚨ	33223	13	4	Stability
Cindy	ᚲᚺᚾᛞᛃ	33718	22	4	Stability
Clare	ᚲᛚᚨᚱᛖ	32394	21	3	Fertility
Cleo	ᚲᛚᛖᛟ	3244	13	4	Stability
Cleopatra	ᚲᛚᛖᛟᛈᚨᛏᚱᚨ	324423393	33	6	Abundance

Girl's name	Rune symbols	Rune numbers	Total	Key number	Key word
Collette	ᚲᛉᚾᛗᛏᛏᛗ	34224334	25	7	Courage
Daisy	ᛗᛁᚾᛋᛁ	13318	16	7	Courage
Dana	ᛗᛁᚾᚠ	1373	14	5	Caution
Darcie	ᛗᛁᚱᚱᚲᛗ	139334	23	5	Caution
Daryl	ᛗᛁᚱᚱᛋᛏ	13982	23	5	Caution
Davina	ᛗᛁᚱᛈᛁᚠ	131373	18	9	Accomplishment
Dawn	ᛗᛁᚱᛃ	1317	12	3	Fertility
Deana	ᛗᛁᛗᚾᚠ	14373	18	9	Accomplishment
Deborah	ᛗᛁᛗᛒᛉᚱᚾᚾ	1434930	24	6	Abundance
Dee	ᛗᛁᛗᛗ	144	9	9	Accomplishment
Delia	ᛗᛁᛗᛏᚠ	14233	13	4	Stability
Di	ᛗᛁ	13	4	4	Stability
Diana	ᛗᛁᚱᚾᚠ	13373	17	8	Dedication
Diane	ᛗᛁᚱᛃᛗ	13374	18	9	Accomplishment
Dido	ᛗᛁᛁᛗᛉ	1314	9	9	Accomplishment
Dina	ᛗᛁᚾᚠ	1373	14	5	Caution
Dione	ᛗᛁᛉᛃᛗ	13474	19	1	Victory
Dolina	ᛗᛁᛉᚾᚠ	142373	20	2	Friendship
Dolores	ᛗᛁᛉᛏᛉᚱᛗᛋ	1424941	25	7	Courage
Donna	ᛗᛁᛉᛃᚠ	14773	22	4	Stability
Doreen	ᛗᛁᛉᚱᛗᛗᛃ	149447	29	2	Friendship
Doris	ᛗᛁᛉᚱᛁᛋ	14931	18	9	Accomplishment
Dorothy	ᛗᛁᛉᚱᛉᛏᚾᛋ	1494308	29	2	Friendship
Drusilla	ᛗᛁᚱᚾᛋᛁᛏᚠ	19713223	28	1	Victory
Dulcie	ᛗᛁᚾᚲᛗ	172334	20	2	Friendship

Girl's name	*Rune symbols*	*Rune numbers*	*Total*	*Key number*	*Key word*
Dyan	ᛞᛇᚨᚾ	1837	19	1	Victory
Eartha	ᛖᚨᚱᛏᚺᚨ	439303	22	4	Stability
Ebony	ᛖᛒᛟᚾᛇ	43478	26	8	Dedication
Eda	ᛖᛞᚨ	413	8	8	Dedication
Edna	ᛖᛞᚾᚨ	4173	15	6	Abundance
Effie	ᛖᚠᚠᛁᛖ	46634	23	5	Caution
Eileen	ᛖᛁᛚᛖᛖᚾ	432447	24	6	Abundance
Eilidh	ᛖᛁᛚᛁᛞᚺ	432310	13	4	Stability
Elaine	ᛖᛚᚨᛁᚾᛖ	423374	23	5	Caution
Eleanor	ᛖᛚᛖᚨᚾᛟᚱ	4243749	33	6	Abundance
Eleanora	ᛖᛚᛖᚨᚾᛟᚱᚨ	42437493	36	9	Accomplishment
Electra	ᛖᛚᛖᚲᛏᚱᚨ	4243393	28	1	Victory
Elena	ᛖᛚᛖᚾᚨ	42473	20	2	Friendship
Eleonora	ᛖᛚᛖᛟᚾᛟᚱᚨ	42447493	37	1	Victory
Elin	ᛖᛚᛁᚾ	4237	16	7	Courage
Elisabeth	ᛖᛚᛁᛊᚨᛒᛖᛏᚺ	423133430	23	5	Caution
Élise	ᛖᛚᛁᛊᛖ	42314	14	5	Caution
Elizabeth	ᛖᛚᛁᛉᚨᛒᛖᛏᚺ	423433430	26	8	Dedication
Elma	ᛖᛚᛗᚨ	4223	11	2	Friendship
Eloise	ᛖᛚᛟᛁᛊᛖ	424314	18	9	Accomplishment
Elva	ᛖᛚᚹᚨ	4213	10	1	Victory
Esther	ᛖᛊᛏᚺᛖᚱ	413049	21	3	Fertility
Ethel	ᛖᛏᚺᛖᛚ	43042	13	4	Stability
Etta	ᛖᛏᛏᚨ	4333	13	4	Stability
Eva	ᛖᚹᚨ	413	8	8	Dedication

Girl's name	*Rune symbols*	*Rune numbers*	*Total*	*Key number*	*Key word*
Fabienne	ᚠᚨᛒᛁᛖᚾᚾᛖ	63334774	37	1	Victory
Fabiola	ᚠᚨᛒᛁᛟᛚᚨ	6333423	24	6	Abundance
Faith	ᚠᚨᛁᛏᚺ	63330	15	6	Abundance
Fatima	ᚠᚨᛏᛁᛗᚨ	633323	20	2	Friendship
Fay	ᚠᚨᛇ	638	17	8	Dedication
Felicia	ᚠᛖᛚᛁᚲᛁᚨ	6423333	24	6	Abundance
Felicity	ᚠᛖᛚᛁᚲᛁᛏᛇ	64233338	32	5	Caution
Fidelia	ᚠᛁᛞᛖᛚᛁᚨ	6314233	22	4	Stability
Fifi	ᚠᛁᚠᛁ	6363	18	9	Accomplishment
Fiona	ᚠᛁᛟᚾᚨ	63473	23	5	Caution
Fleur	ᚠᛚᛖᚢᚱ	62479	28	1	Victory
Flo	ᚠᛚᛟ	624	12	3	Fertility
Flora	ᚠᛚᛟᚱᚨ	62493	24	6	Abundance
Flower	ᚠᛚᛟᚹᛖᚱ	624149	26	8	Dedication
Fortune	ᚠᛟᚱᛏᚢᚾᛖ	6493774	40	4	Stability
Fran	ᚠᚱᚨᚾ	6937	25	7	Courage
Frances	ᚠᚱᚨᚾᚲᛖᛊ	6937341	33	6	Abundance
Francesca	ᚠᚱᚨᚾᚲᛖᛊᚲᚨ	693734133	39	3	Fertility
Francie	ᚠᚱᚨᚾᚲᛁᛖ	6937334	35	8	Dedication
Francine	ᚠᚱᚨᚾᚲᛁᚾᛖ	69373374	42	6	Abundance
Francisca	ᚠᚱᚨᚾᚲᛁᛊᚲᚨ	693733133	38	2	Friendship
Freda	ᚠᚱᛖᛞᚨ	69413	23	5	Caution
Freya	ᚠᚱᛖᛇᚨ	69483	30	3	Fertility
Gabbie	ᚷᚨᛒᛒᛁᛖ	633334	22	4	Stability
Gabrielle	ᚷᚨᛒᚱᛁᛖᛚᛚᛖ	633934224	36	9	Accomplishment

Girl's name	Rune symbols	Rune numbers	Total	Key number	Key word
Gaia	ᚷᚨᚠ	6333	15	6	Abundance
Gardenia	ᚷᚨᚱᛞᛁᛗᚺᚠ	63914733	36	9	Accomplishment
Gayle	ᚷᚨᚾᛏᛗ	63824	23	5	Caution
Gaynor	ᚷᚨᚾᛈᛟᚱ	638749	37	1	Victory
Gemma	ᚷᛗᛈᛈᛈᚨ	64223	17	8	Dedication
Genevieve	ᚷᛗᚾᛁᛈᛁᛈᛈ	647413414	34	7	Courage
Georgia	ᚷᛗᛟᚱᚷᛁᚠ	6449633	35	8	Dedication
Geraldine	ᚷᛗᚱᚨᛝᛞᛁᚺᛗ	649321374	39	3	Fertility
Gertrude	ᚷᛗᚱᛏᚱᛝᛞᛁᛗ	64939714	43	7	Courage
Gigi	ᚷᛁᚷᛁ	6363	18	9	Accomplishment
Gilda	ᚷᛁᚾᛞᚠ	63213	15	6	Abundance
Gill	ᚷᛁᚾ	6322	13	4	Stability
Gillian	ᚷᛁᚾᚾᛁᚾ	6322337	26	8	Dedication
Ginnie	ᚷᛁᚺᚾᛁᛗ	637734	30	3	Fertility
Giovanna	ᚷᛁᛟᛈᚾᚾᚨ	63413773	34	7	Courage
Gisela	ᚷᛁᛊᛗᚾᚠ	631423	19	1	Victory
Gladys	ᚷᚾᚾᛞᚾᛊ	623181	21	3	Fertility
Gleda	ᚷᚾᛗᛞᚠ	62413	16	7	Courage
Glenda	ᚷᚾᛗᚺᛞᚠ	624713	23	5	Caution
Glenys	ᚷᚾᛗᚺᚾᛊ	624781	28	1	Victory
Gloria	ᚷᚾᛟᚱᛁᚠ	624933	27	9	Accomplishment
Glynis	ᚷᚾᚾᚺᛊ	628731	27	9	Accomplishment
Golda	ᚷᛟᚾᛞᚠ	64213	16	7	Courage
Goldie	ᚷᛟᚾᛞᛁᛗ	642134	20	2	Friendship
Grace	ᚷᚱᚱᚲᛗ	69334	25	7	Courage

Girl's name	Rune symbols	Rune numbers	Total	Key number	Key word
Greta	ᚷᚱᛖᛏᚨ	69433	25	7	Courage
Gwenda	ᚷᛈᛖᚺᛞᚨ	614713	22	4	Stability
Gwyneth	ᚷᛈᛱᛉᛏᚺ	6187430	29	2	Friendship
Halcyon	ᚺᚨᛈᚲᛃᛈ	323847	27	9	Accomplishment
Hannah	ᚺᚨᚺᚺ	37730	20	2	Friendship
Haralda	ᚺᚨᚱᚨᛞᚨ	393213	21	3	Fertility
Harmony	ᚺᚱᚱᛗᛈᛏ	392478	33	6	Abundance
Hattie	ᚺᚨᛏᛏᛁ	33334	16	7	Courage
Hayley	ᚺᚨᛃᛗᛃ	38248	25	7	Courage
Hazel	ᚺᚨᛉᛖᛏ	3442	13	4	Stability
Heather	ᚺᛖᚨᛏᚺᛖᚱ	433049	23	5	Caution
Hebe	ᚺᛖᛒᛖ	434	11	2	Friendship
Hedda	ᚺᛖᛞᛞᚨ	4113	9	9	Accomplishment
Heidi	ᚺᛖᛁᛞᛁ	4313	11	2	Friendship
Helen	ᚺᛖᛏᛏᚺ	4247	17	8	Dedication
Helene	ᚺᛖᛏᛏᚺᛖ	42474	21	3	Fertility
Henrietta	ᚺᛖᚺᚱᛖᛏᛏᚨ	47934333	36	9	Accomplishment
Hera	ᚺᛖᚱᚨ	493	16	7	Courage
Herta	ᚺᛖᚱᛏᚨ	4933	19	1	Victory
Hertha	ᚺᛖᚱᛏᚺ	49303	19	1	Victory
Hibernia	ᚺᛒᛖᚱᚺ	3349733	32	5	Caution
Hilary	ᚺᛁᚱᚱᛃ	32398	25	7	Courage
Hilda	ᚺᛁᛞᚨ	3213	9	9	Accomplishment
Hildegarde	ᚺᛁᛞᛖᛗᚷᚱᛞᛖᛗ	321463914	33	6	Abundance
Holly	ᚺᛈᛏᛃ	4228	16	7	Courage

Book of Runes

Girl's name	Rune symbols	Rune numbers	Total	Key number	Key word
Honey	ᚻᚩᛏᛗᛋ	4748	23	5	Caution
Honour	ᚻᚩᛏᚩᚾᚱ	47479	31	4	Stability
Hope	ᚻᚩᛁᛗ	424	10	1	Victory
Hyacinth	ᚻᛄᛈᚳᛁᛏᚾ	8333730	27	9	Accomplishment
Ida	ᛁᛈᚨ	313	7	7	Courage
Ilona	ᛁᛚᚩᛏᚨ	32473	19	1	Victory
Imogen	ᛁᛗᚩᚷᛗᛁ	324647	26	8	Dedication
Ina	ᛁᚾᚨ	373	13	4	Stability
India	ᛁᚾᛈᚳᚨ	37133	17	8	Dedication
Inga	ᛁᚾᚷᚨ	3763	19	1	Victory
Innes	ᛁᚾᛏᛗᛋ	37741	22	4	Stability
Iola	ᛁᚩᛏᚨ	3423	12	3	Fertility
Iolanthe	ᛁᚩᛏᚾᛏᛏᚾᛗ	34237304	26	8	Dedication
Iole	ᛁᚩᛏᛗ	3424	13	4	Stability
Iona	ᛁᚩᛏᚨ	3473	17	8	Dedication
Irene	ᚱᛗᛏᛗ	39474	27	9	Accomplishment
Iris	ᚱᛁᛋ	3931	16	7	Courage
Irma	ᚱᛈᛗᚨ	3923	17	8	Dedication
Isa	ᛁᛋᚨ	313	7	7	Courage
Isabel	ᛁᛋᚨᛒᛗᛏ	313342	16	7	Courage
Isabelle	ᛁᛋᚨᛒᛗᛏᛗᛗ	31334224	22	4	Stability
Isadora	ᛁᛋᚨᛈᚳᚩᚱᚨ	3131493	24	6	Abundance
Ishbel	ᛁᛋᚾᛒᛗᛏ	310342	13	4	Stability
Isidora	ᛁᛋᛁᚳᚩᚱᚨ	3131493	24	6	Abundance
Isobel	ᛁᛋᚩᛒᛗᛏ	314342	17	8	Dedication

Girl's name	Rune symbols	Rune numbers	Total	Key number	Key word
Isolde	ᛁᛋᚱᚾᛉᛖ	314214	15	6	Abundance
Ivana	ᛁᛩᚾᚨ	31373	17	8	Dedication
Ivy	ᛁᚾ	318	12	3	Fertility
Izzie	ᛁᛃᛃᛖ	34434	18	9	Accomplishment
Jade	ᛃᚨᛉᛖ	8314	16	7	Courage
Jamesina	ᛃᚨᛗᛖᛋᛁᚨ	83241373	31	4	Stability
Janet	ᛃᚨᚾᛖᛏ	83743	25	7	Courage
Janine	ᛃᚨᚾᛁᚾᛖ	837374	32	5	Caution
Jasmine	ᛃᚨᛋᛗᛁᚾᛖ	8312374	28	1	Victory
Jayne	ᛃᚨᚾᛃᛖ	83874	30	3	Fertility
Jean	ᛃᛖᚨᚾ	8437	22	4	Stability
Jeanette	ᛃᛖᚨᚾᛖᛏᛏᛖ	84374334	36	9	Accomplishment
Jenna	ᛃᛖᚾᚾᚨ	84773	29	2	Friendship
Jennifer	ᛃᛖᚾᚾᛁᚠᛖᚱ	84773649	48	3	Fertility
Jenny	ᛃᛖᚾᚾᛃ	84778	34	7	Courage
Jessie	ᛃᛖᛋᛋᛁᛖ	841134	21	3	Fertility
Jewel	ᛃᛖᚹᛖᛏ	84142	19	1	Victory
Jezebel	ᛃᛖᛃᛖᛒᛖᛏ	8444342	29	2	Friendship
Joan	ᛃᛟᚨᚾ	8437	22	4	Stability
Jodie	ᛃᛟᛉᛁᛖ	84134	20	2	Friendship
Jordana	ᛃᛟᚱᛉᚨᚾᚨ	8491373	35	8	Dedication
Josephine	ᛃᛟᛋᛖᛈᚺᛁᚾᛖ	841420374	33	6	Abundance
Josie	ᛃᛟᛋᛁᛖ	84134	20	2	Friendship
Joy	ᛃᛟᚾ	848	20	2	Friendship
Joyce	ᛃᛟᚾᚲᛖ	84834	27	9	Accomplishment

Girl's name	Rune symbols	Rune numbers	Total	Key number	Key word
Judy	ᛋᚾᛤᛋ	8718	24	6	Abundance
Julia	ᛋᚾᚾᚠ	87233	23	5	Caution
Juliana	ᛋᚾᚾᚠᚢ	8723373	33	6	Abundance
Julie	ᛋᚾᚾᛗ	87234	24	6	Abundance
Julienne	ᛋᚾᚾᛗᚢᛗ	87234774	42	6	Abundance
Juliette	ᛋᚾᚾᛗᛏᛏᛗ	87234334	34	7	Courage
Juno	ᛋᚾᛤᛝ	8774	26	8	Dedication
Justina	ᛋᚾᛊᛏᚢᚠ	8713373	32	5	Caution
Justine	ᛋᚾᛊᛏᚢᛗ	8713374	33	6	Abundance
Karen	ᚲᚠᚱᛗᚢ	33947	26	8	Dedication
Kate	ᚲᚠᛏᛗ	3334	13	4	Stability
Katerina	ᚲᚠᛏᛗᚱᚢᚠ	33349373	35	8	Dedication
Kath	ᚲᚠᛏᚾ	3330	9	9	Accomplishment
Katherine	ᚲᚠᛏᚾᛗᚱᚢᛗ	333049374	36	9	Accomplishment
Kathleen	ᚲᚠᛏᚾᛗᛗᚢ	33302447	26	8	Dedication
Kathryn	ᚲᚠᛏᚾᚱᛊᚢ	3330987	33	6	Abundance
Katie	ᚲᚠᛏᛗ	33334	16	7	Courage
Katriona	ᚲᚠᛏᚱᛁᛝᚠ	33393473	35	8	Dedication
Keely	ᚲᛗᛗᛋ	34428	21	3	Fertility
Keira	ᚲᛁᚱᚠ	34393	22	4	Stability
Kelly	ᚲᛗᛏᛋ	34228	19	1	Victory
Kendra	ᚲᛗᚢᛤᚱᚠ	347193	27	9	Accomplishment
Kenya	ᚲᛗᚢᚠ	34783	25	7	Courage
Kerry	ᚲᛗᚱᚱᛋ	34998	33	6	Abundance
Kim	ᚲᛈᛗ	332	8	8	Dedication

Name and Numerology

Girl's name	Rune symbols	Rune numbers	Total	Key number	Key word
Kimberley	ᚲᛁᛗᛒᛖᚱᚾᛖᛃ	332349248	38	2	Friendship
Kittie	ᚲᛁᛏᛏᛁᛗ	333334	19	1	Victory
Kizzie	ᚲᛃᛃᛁᛗ	334434	21	3	Fertility
Klara	ᚲᛚᚱᚨ	32393	20	2	Friendship
Kristen	ᚲᚱᛁᛋᛏᛗᚺ	3931347	30	3	Fertility
Kristie	ᚲᚱᛁᛋᛏᛁᛗ	3931334	26	8	Dedication
Kristin	ᚲᚱᛁᛋᛏᚺ	3931337	29	2	Friendship
Kristina	ᚲᚱᛁᛋᛏᚺᚨ	39313373	32	5	Caution
Kylie	ᚲᛃᛁᛗ	38234	20	2	Friendship
Lacey	ᛚᚨᚲᛃ	23348	20	2	Friendship
Lana	ᛚᚨᚺᚨ	2373	15	6	Abundance
Lara	ᛚᚱᚨ	2393	17	8	Dedication
Latisha	ᛚᚨᛏᛁᛋᚾᚨ	2333103	15	6	Abundance
Laura	ᛚᚨᚢᚱᚨ	23793	24	6	Abundance
Laurel	ᛚᚨᚢᚱᛗᛏ	237942	27	9	Accomplishment
Lauren	ᛚᚨᚢᚱᛗᚺ	237947	32	5	Caution
Lavender	ᛚᚨᚡᛗᚺᛞᛇᛗᚱ	23147149	31	4	Stability
Lavinia	ᛚᚨᚡᛁᚺᚨ	2313733	22	4	Stability
Leah	ᛚᛗᚨᚺ	2430	9	9	Accomplishment
Leanne	ᛚᛗᚨᚺᚾᛗ	243774	27	9	Accomplishment
Leanora	ᛚᛗᚨᚺᛇᚱᚨ	2437493	32	5	Caution
Leaona	ᛚᛗᚨᛇᚺᚨ	243473	23	5	Caution
Leonora	ᛚᛗᛇᚺᛇᚱᚨ	2447493	33	6	Abundance
Lesley	ᛚᛗᛋᛗᛃ	241248	21	3	Fertility
Leslie	ᛚᛗᛋᛁᛗ	241234	16	7	Courage

Girl's name	Rune symbols	Rune numbers	Total	Key number	Key word
Leticia	ᛗᛖᛏᚲᛁᚨ	2433333	21	3	Fertility
Lexie	ᛗᛖᚦᛁᛗ	24534	18	9	Accomplishment
Libby	ᛗᛒᛒᛋ	23338	19	1	Victory
Lil	ᛗᛁ	232	7	7	Courage
Lilac	ᛗᛁᚨᚲ	23233	13	4	Stability
Lilah	ᛗᛁᚨᚾ	23230	10	1	Victory
Lili	ᛗᛁ	2323	10	1	Victory
Lilian	ᛗᛁᚨᛣ	232337	20	2	Friendship
Lilie	ᛗᛁᛗ	23234	14	5	Caution
Lilith	ᛗᛁᛏᚾ	232330	13	4	Stability
Linnette	ᚾᛣᛗᛏᛏᛗ	23774334	33	6	Abundance
Linsay	ᚾᛣᛋᚱᛋ	237138	24	6	Abundance
Liz	ᛗᛉ	234	9	9	Accomplishment
Lizbeth	ᚾᛉᛒᛗᛏᚾ	2343430	19	1	Victory
Lois	ᛚᛈᛁᛋ	2431	10	1	Victory
Loretta	ᛚᛈᛗᛏᛏᚨ	2494333	28	1	Victory
Lorna	ᛚᛈᚱᛡ	24973	25	7	Courage
Lorraine	ᛚᛈᚱᚱᚾᛗ	24993374	41	5	Caution
Lucille	ᛗᚲᛁᛗᛗ	2733224	23	5	Caution
Lucy	ᛗᚲᛋ	2738	20	2	Friendship
Lulu	ᛗᛗᛗ	2727	18	9	Accomplishment
Lynette	ᛚᛣᛗᛏᛏᛗ	2874334	31	4	Stability
Mabel	ᛈᚱᛒᛗᛏ	23342	14	5	Caution
Madalena	ᛈᚱᛈᛪᛣᛗᛈ	23132473	25	7	Courage
Madeleine	ᛈᚱᛈᛪᛗᛗᛈᛗ	231424374	30	3	Fertility

Girl's name	Rune symbols	Rune numbers	Total	Key number	Key word
Madge	ᛗᚨᛞᚷᛖ	23164	16	7	Courage
Madonna	ᛗᚨᛞᛟᚾᚾᚨ	2314773	27	9	Accomplishment
Margaret	ᛗᚨᚱᚷᚨᚱᛖᛏ	23963943	39	3	Fertility
Maria	ᛗᚨᚱᛁᚨ	23933	20	2	Friendship
Marian	ᛗᚨᚱᛁᚨᚾ	239337	27	9	Accomplishment
Martha	ᛗᚨᚱᛏᚺᚨ	239303	20	2	Friendship
Marti	ᛗᚨᚱᛏᛁ	23933	20	2	Friendship
Mary	ᛗᚨᚱᛃ	239800	22	4	Stability
Maryann	ᛗᚨᚱᛃᚨᚾᚾ	2398377	39	3	Fertility
Marylou	ᛗᚨᚱᛃᛚᛟᚢ	2398247	35	8	Dedication
Matilde	ᛗᚨᛏᛁᛚᛞᛖ	2333214	18	9	Accomplishment
Maureen	ᛗᚨᚢᚱᛖᛖᚾ	2379447	36	9	Accomplishment
Mavis	ᛗᚨᚢᛁᛊ	23131	10	1	Victory
Megan	ᛗᛖᚷᚨᚾ	24637	22	4	Stability
Melinda	ᛗᛖᛚᛁᚾᛞᚨ	2423713	22	4	Stability
Melissa	ᛗᛖᛚᛁᛊᛊᚨ	2423113	16	7	Courage
Melody	ᛗᛖᛚᛟᛞᛃ	242418	21	3	Fertility
Mercy	ᛗᛖᚱᚲᛃ	24938	26	8	Dedication
Meryl	ᛗᛖᚱᛃᛚ	24982	25	7	Courage
Millicent	ᛗᛁᛚᛚᛁᚲᛖᚾᛏ	232233473	29	2	Friendship
Minerva	ᛗᛁᚾᛖᚱᚡᚨ	2374913	29	2	Friendship
Miriam	ᛗᛁᚱᛁᚨᛗ	239332	22	4	Stability
Moira	ᛗᛟᛁᚱᚨ	24393	21	3	Fertility
Monica	ᛗᛟᚾᛁᚲᚨ	247333	22	4	Stability
Morag	ᛗᛟᚱᚨᚷ	24936	24	6	Abundance

Girl's name	Rune symbols	Rune numbers	Total	Key number	Key word
Moyra	ᛗᛟᛃᚱᚠ	24893	26	8	Dedication
Myrna	ᛗᛃᚱᚴᚠ	28973	29	2	Friendship
Nadia	ᚼᚾᛞᛉᚢ	73133	17	8	Dedication
Nadine	ᚼᚾᛞᛉᛁᛗ	731374	25	7	Courage
Nan	ᚼᚠᚾ	737	17	8	Dedication
Nancy	ᚼᚠᚾᚲᛃ	73738	28	1	Victory
Naomi	ᚼᚠᛟᛗᛁ	73423	19	1	Victory
Natalie	ᚾᚠᛏᚾᛗᛗ	7333234	25	7	Courage
Natasha	ᚾᚠᛏᚱᛊᚾᚠ	7333103	20	2	Friendship
Nebula	ᚼᛗᛒᚾᚾᚠ	743723	26	8	Dedication
Nell	ᚼᛗᛏᛏ	7422	15	6	Abundance
Nerys	ᚼᛗᚱᛃᛊ	74981	29	2	Friendship
Nessie	ᚼᛗᛊᛊᛁᛗ	741134	20	2	Friendship
Nesta	ᚼᛗᛊᛏᚠ	74133	18	9	Accomplishment
Netta	ᚼᛗᛏᛏᛏᚠ	74333	20	2	Friendship
Nicole	ᚼᚲᛟᛟᛗ	733424	23	5	Caution
Nikki	ᚼᚲᚲᛁ	73333	19	1	Victory
Nina	ᚼᛁᚾᚠ	7373	20	2	Friendship
Noël	ᛁᛟᛗᛏ	7442	17	8	Dedication
Noëlle	ᛁᛟᛗᛏᛏᛗ	744224	23	5	Caution
Nora	ᛁᛟᚱᚠ	7493	23	5	Caution
Noreen	ᛁᛟᚱᛗᛗᛁ	749447	35	8	Dedication
Norma	ᛁᛟᚱᛗᚠ	74923	25	7	Courage
Nuala	ᚼᛁᚾᚠ	77323	22	4	Stability
Octavia	ᛟᚲᛏᚾᛈᛁᚠ	4333133	20	2	Friendship

Girl's name	*Rune symbols*	*Rune numbers*	*Total*	*Key number*	*Key word*
Odelia	ᛟᛞᛖᛚᛁᚨ	414233	17	8	Dedication
Odette	ᛟᛞᛖᛏᛏᛖ	414334	19	1	Victory
Odile	ᛟᛞᛁᛚᛖ	41324	14	5	Caution
Olga	ᛟᛚᚷᚨ	4263	15	6	Abundance
Olimpia	ᛟᛚᛁᛗᛈᛁᚨ	4232233	19	1	Victory
Olivia	ᛟᛚᛁᚹᛁᚨ	423133	16	7	Courage
Olwen	ᛟᛚᚹᛖᚾ	42147	18	9	Accomplishment
Olympia	ᛟᛚᛇᛗᛈᛁᚨ	4282233	24	6	Abundance
Oona	ᛟᛟᚾᚨ	4473	18	9	Accomplishment
Opal	ᛟᛈᚨᛚ	4232	11	2	Friendship
Ophelia	ᛟᛈᚺᛖᛚᛁᚨ	4204233	18	9	Accomplishment
Oprah	ᛟᛈᚱᚨᚺ	42930	18	9	Accomplishment
Oriana	ᛟᚱᛁᚨᚾᚨ	493373	29	2	Friendship
Oriel	ᛟᚱᛁᛖᛚ	49342	22	4	Stability
Orla	ᛟᚱᛚᚨ	4923	18	9	Accomplishment
Orlanda	ᛟᚱᛚᚨᚾᛞᚨ	4923713	29	2	Friendship
Orna	ᛟᚱᚾᚨ	4973	23	5	Caution
Ortensia	ᛟᚱᛏᛖᚾᛊᛁᚨ	49347133	34	7	Courage
Ottavia	ᛟᛏᛏᚨᚹᛁᚨ	4333133	20	2	Friendship
Paige	ᛈᚨᛁᚷᛖ	23364	18	9	Accomplishment
Paloma	ᛈᚨᛚᛟᛗᚨ	232423	16	7	Courage
Pandora	ᛈᚨᚾᛞᛟᚱᚨ	2371493	29	2	Friendship
Pansy	ᛈᚨᚾᛊᛇ	23718	21	3	Fertility
Patience	ᛈᚨᛏᛁᛖᚾᚲᛖ	23334734	29	2	Friendship
Patricia	ᛈᚨᛏᚱᛁᚲᛁᚨ	23393333	29	2	Friendship

Girl's name	Rune symbols	Rune numbers	Total	Key number	Key word
Patsy	ᚲᛐᛏᛋᛌ	23318	17	8	Dedication
Pattie	ᚲᛐᛏᛏᛁᛖ	233334	18	9	Accomplishment
Paula	ᚲᛐᚢᛐ	23723	17	8	Dedication
Paulette	ᚲᛐᚢᛁᛏᛏᛁᛖ	23724334	28	1	Victory
Peace	ᚲᛖᛐᚲᛖ	24334	16	7	Courage
Pearl	ᚲᛖᛐᛐᛌ	24392	20	2	Friendship
Penelope	ᚲᛖᛁᛖᛏᛒᚲᛖ	24742424	29	2	Friendship
Penny	ᚲᛖᛁᛁᛌ	24778	28	1	Victory
Peony	ᚲᛖᛒᛁᛌ	24478	25	7	Courage
Perdita	ᚲᛖᛐᛞᚲᛁᛏᛐ	2491333	25	7	Courage
Persephone	ᚲᛖᛐᛋᛖᚲᛖᛒᛁᛖᛏ	2491420474	37	1	Victory
Persis	ᚲᛖᛐᛋᛁᛋ	249131	20	2	Friendship
Petra	ᚲᛖᛏᛏᛐᛐ	24393	21	3	Fertility
Petrina	ᚲᛖᛏᛏᛐᛁᛁᛐ	2439373	31	4	Stability
Petula	ᚲᛖᛏᛏᛁᛁᛐ	243723	21	3	Fertility
Petunia	ᚲᛖᛏᛏᛁᛁᛁᛐ	2437733	29	2	Friendship
Phebe	ᚲᛁᛁᛒᛖᛏ	20434	13	4	Stability
Philippa	ᚲᛁᛁᛁᚲᚲᛐ	20323223	17	8	Dedication
Philomena	ᚲᛁᛁᛁᛒᛜᛏᛐᛁᛐ	203242473	27	9	Accomplishment
Phoebe	ᚲᛁᛒᛒᛖᛒᛖ	204434	17	8	Dedication
Phyllis	ᚲᛁᛌᛏᛏᛌᛋ	2082231	18	9	Accomplishment
Pia	ᚲᛁᛐ	233	8	8	Dedication
Pilar	ᚲᛁᛁᛐᛐ	23239	19	1	Victory
Pippa	ᚲᚲᚲᛐ	23223	12	3	Fertility
Polly	ᚲᛒᛏᛏᛌ	24228	18	9	Accomplishment

Girl's name	*Rune symbols*	*Rune numbers*	*Total*	*Key number*	*Key word*
Pollyanna	ᛈᛟᛚᛚᛇᚨᚾᚾᚨ	242283773	38	2	Friendship
Primrose	ᛈᚱᛁᛗᚱᛟᛊᛖ	29329414	34	7	Courage
Prunella	ᛈᚱᚢᚾᛖᛚᛚᚨ	29774223	36	9	Accomplishment
Psyche	ᛈᛊᛇᚲᚺᛖ	218304	18	9	Accomplishment
Queenie	ᛜᚢᛖᛖᚾᛁᛖ	6744734	35	8	Dedication
Quenby	ᛜᚢᛖᚾᛒᛇ	674738	35	8	Dedication
Rachel	ᚱᚨᚲᚺᛖᛚ	933042	21	3	Fertility
Rae	ᚱᚨᛖ	934	16	7	Courage
Raisa	ᚱᚨᛁᛊᚨ	93313	19	1	Victory
Raphaela	ᚱᚨᛈᚺᚨᛖᛚᚨ	93203423	26	8	Dedication
Raquel	ᚱᚨᛜᚢᛖᛚ	936742	31	4	Stability
Raven	ᚱᚨᚹᛖᚾ	93147	24	6	Abundance
Rayne	ᚱᚨᛇᚾᛖ	93874	31	4	Stability
Rea	ᚱᛖᚨ	943	16	7	Courage
Rebecca	ᚱᛖᛒᛖᚲᚲᚨ	9434333	29	2	Friendship
Regina	ᚱᛖᚷᛁᚾᚨ	946373	32	5	Caution
Reine	ᚱᛖᛁᚾᛖ	94374	27	9	Accomplishment
Renata	ᚱᛖᚾᚨᛏᚨ	947333	29	2	Friendship
Renee	ᚱᛖᚾᛖᛖ	94744	28	1	Victory
Rhea	ᚱᚺᛖᚨ	9043	16	7	Courage
Rhiannon	ᚱᚺᛁᚨᚾᚾᛟᚾ	90337747	40	4	Stability
Rhona	ᚱᚺᛟᚾᚨ	90473	23	5	Caution
Rita	ᚱᛁᛏᚨ	9333	18	9	Accomplishment
Roasnne	ᚱᛟᚨᛊᚾᚾᛖ	9431774	35	8	Dedication
Roberta	ᚱᛟᛒᛖᚱᛏᚨ	9434933	35	8	Dedication

Girl's name	Rune symbols	Rune numbers	Total	Key number	Key word
Robina	ᚱᛟᛒᛁᚻᚨ	943373	29	2	Friendship
Rochelle	ᚱᛟᚲᚾᛗᛏᛗ	94304224	28	1	Victory
Rosalie	ᚱᛟᛋᚨᛁᛗ	9413234	26	8	Dedication
Rosalind	ᚱᛟᛋᚨᛁᚻᛉ	94132371	30	3	Fertility
Rose	ᚱᛟᛋᛗ	9414	18	9	Accomplishment
Roseanne	ᚱᛟᛋᛗᚨᚻᛗ	94143774	39	3	Fertility
Rosemarie	ᚱᛟᛋᛗᛈᚨᚱᛁᛗ	941423934	39	3	Fertility
Rosemary	ᚱᛟᛋᛗᛈᚨᚱᛋ	94142398	40	4	Stability
Rosetta	ᚱᛟᛋᛗᛏᛏᚨ	9414333	27	9	Accomplishment
Rosie	ᚱᛟᛋᛁᛗ	94134	21	3	Fertility
Rowena	ᚱᛟᛈᛗᚻᚨ	941473	28	1	Victory
Roxanne	ᚱᛟᛒᚨᛋᛗ	9453774	39	3	Fertility
Ruth	ᚱᛗᛏᚾ	9730000	19	1	Victory
Sally	ᛋᚨᛏᛋ	13228	16	7	Courage
Salome	ᛋᚨᛋᛟᛈᛗ	13242400	16	7	Courage
Salvia	ᛋᚨᛈᛈᛁᚱ	132133	13	4	Stability
Samantha	ᛋᛈᚨᚻᛏᛏᚾᚨ	13237303	22	4	Stability
Sapphire	ᛋᚨᛇᛁᚾᛁᚱᛗ	13220394	24	6	Abundance
Sarah	ᛋᚨᚱᚨᚾ	13930	16	7	Courage
Scarlett	ᛋᚲᚨᚱᛗᛏᛏᛏ	13392433	28	1	Victory
Selina	ᛋᛗᛏᚻᚨ	142373	20	2	Friendship
Senga	ᛋᛗᚻᚷᚨ	14763	21	3	Fertility
Seonaid	ᛋᛗᛟᚻᛁᛉ	1447331	23	5	Caution
Seraphina	ᛋᛗᚱᚨᚲᚾᚻᚨ	149320373	32	5	Caution
Shannon	ᛋᚻᚨᚻᛟᛏ	1037747	29	2	Friendship

Girl's name	*Rune symbols*	*Rune numbers*	*Total*	*Key number*	*Key word*
Sharon	ᛊᚺᚨᚱᛟᚾ	103947	24	6	Abundance
Sheelagh	ᛊᚺᛖᛖᛚᚨᚷᚺ	10442360	20	2	Friendship
Sheena	ᛊᚺᛖᛖᚾᚨ	104473	19	1	Victory
Sheila	ᛊᚺᛖᛁᛚᚨ	104323	13	4	Stability
Sheryl	ᛊᚺᛖᚱᛇᛚ	104982	24	6	Abundance
Shirley	ᛊᚺᛁᚱᛚᛖᛇ	1039248	27	9	Accomplishment
Shona	ᛊᚺᛟᚾᚨ	10473	15	6	Abundance
Sian	ᛊᛁᚨᚾ	1337	14	5	Caution
Sibyl	ᛊᛁᛒᛇᛚ	13382	17	8	Dedication
Sidonia	ᛊᛁᛞᛟᚾᛁᚨ	1314733	22	4	Stability
Sigrid	ᛊᛁᚷᚱᛁᛞ	136931	23	5	Caution
Silvana	ᛊᛁᛚᚹᚨᚾᚨ	1321373	20	2	Friendship
Silvia	ᛊᛁᛚᚹᛁᚨ	132133	13	4	Stability
Simone	ᛊᛁᛗᛟᚾᛖ	132474	21	3	Fertility
Sinead	ᛊᛁᚾᛖᚨᛞ	137431	19	1	Victory
Siobhan	ᛊᛁᛟᛒᚺᚨᚾ	1343037	21	3	Fertility
Sofie	ᛊᛟᚠᛁᛖ	14634	18	9	Accomplishment
Sonya	ᛊᛟᚾᛇᚨ	14783	23	5	Caution
Sophia	ᛊᛟᛈᚺᛁᚨ	142033	13	4	Stability
Soraya	ᛊᛟᚱᚨᛇᚨ	149383	28	1	Victory
Star	ᛊᛏᚨᚱ	1339	16	7	Courage
Stella	ᛊᛏᛖᛚᛚᚨ	134223	15	6	Abundance
Stephanie	ᛊᛏᛖᛈᚺᚨᚾᛁᛖ	134203734	27	9	Accomplishment
Storm	ᛊᛏᛟᚱᛗ	13492	19	1	Victory
Summer	ᛊᚢᛗᛗᛖᚱ	172249	25	7	Courage

Girl's name	*Rune symbols*	*Rune numbers*	*Total*	*Key number*	*Key word*
Susan	ᛊᚢᛊᚨᚾ	17137	19	1	Victory
Sybyl	ᛊᛇᛒᛇᛚ	18382	22	4	Stability
Sylvia	ᛊᛇᛚᚹᛁᚨ	182133	18	9	Accomplishment
Tabitha	ᛏᚨᛒᛁᛏᚺᚨ	3333303	18	9	Accomplishment
Tallulah	ᛏᚨᛚᛚᚢᛚᚨᚺ	33227230	22	4	Stability
Tamara	ᛏᚨᛗᚨᚱᚨ	332393	23	5	Caution
Tammie	ᛏᚨᛗᛗᛁᛖ	332234	17	8	Dedication
Tamsin	ᛏᚨᛗᛊᛁᚾ	332137	19	1	Victory
Tansy	ᛏᚨᚾᛊᛇ	33718	22	4	Stability
Tara	ᛏᚨᚱᚨ	3393	18	9	Accomplishment
Tatiana	ᛏᚨᛏᛁᚨᚾᚨ	3333373	25	7	Courage
Tempest	ᛏᛖᛗᛈᛖᛊᛏ	3422413	19	1	Victory
Teresa	ᛏᛖᚱᛖᛊᚨ	349413	24	6	Abundance
Teri	ᛏᛖᚱᛁ	3493	19	1	Victory
Tess	ᛏᛖᛊᛊ	3411	9	9	Accomplishment
Thea	ᛏᚺᛖᚨ	3043	10	1	Victory
Thelma	ᛏᚺᛖᛚᛗᚨ	304223	14	5	Caution
Theodora	ᛏᚺᛖᛟᛞᛟᚱᚨ	30441493	28	1	Victory
Theresa	ᛏᚺᛖᚱᛖᛊᚨ	3049413	24	6	Abundance
Thomasina	ᛏᚺᛟᛗᚨᛊᛁᚾᚨ	304231373	26	8	Dedication
Tiffany	ᛏᛁᚠᚠᚨᚾᛇ	3366378	36	9	Accomplishment
Tilly	ᛏᛁᛚᛚᛇ	33228	18	9	Accomplishment
Tina	ᛏᛁᚾᚨ	3373	16	7	Courage
Titania	ᛏᛁᛏᚨᚾᛁᚨ	3333733	25	7	Courage
Tonia	ᛏᛟᚾᛁᚨ	34733	20	2	Friendship

Girl's name	*Rune symbols*	*Rune numbers*	*Total*	*Key number*	*Key word*
Topaz	ᛏᛟᛈᚨᛉ	34234	16	7	Courage
Tracie	ᛏᚱᚨᚲᛁᛖ	393334	25	7	Courage
Trisha	ᛏᚱᛁᛊᚺᚨ	393103	19	1	Victory
Trista	ᛏᚱᛁᛊᛏᚨ	393133	22	4	Stability
Tuesday	ᛏᚢᛖᛊᛞᚨᛇ	3741138	27	9	Accomplishment
Ulrica	ᚢᛚᚱᛁᚲᚨ	729333	27	9	Accomplishment
Una	ᚢᚾᚨ	773	17	8	Dedication
Ursula	ᚢᚱᛊᚢᛚᚨ	791723	29	2	Friendship
Valentina	ᚹᚨᛚᛖᚾᛏᛁᚾᚨ	132473373	33	6	Abundance
Valerie	ᚹᚨᛚᛖᚱᛁᛖ	1324934	26	8	Dedication
Vanessa	ᚹᚨᚾᛖᛊᛊᚨ	1374113	20	2	Friendship
Velvet	ᚹᛖᛚᚹᛖᛏ	142143	15	6	Abundance
Vera	ᚹᛖᚱᚨ	1493	17	8	Dedication
Verity	ᚹᛖᚱᛁᛏᛇ	149338	28	1	Victory
Verona	ᚹᛖᚱᛟᚾᚨ	149473	28	1	Victory
Veronica	ᚹᛖᚱᛟᚾᛁᚲᚨ	14947333	34	7	Courage
Vicki	ᚹᛁᚲᚲᛁ	13333	13	4	Stability
Victoria	ᚹᛁᚲᛏᛟᚱᛁᚨ	13334933	29	2	Friendship
Vilma	ᚹᛁᛚᛗᚨ	13223	11	2	Friendship
Viola	ᚹᛁᛟᛚᚨ	13423	13	4	Stability
Violetta	ᚹᛁᛟᛚᛖᛏᛏᚨ	13424333	23	5	Caution
Virginia	ᚹᛁᚱᚷᛁᚾᛁᚨ	13963733	35	8	Dedication
Wanda	ᚹᚨᚾᛞᚨ	13713	15	6	Abundance
Wenda	ᚹᛖᚾᛞᚨ	14713	16	7	Courage
Wendy	ᚹᛖᚾᛞᛇ	14718	21	3	Fertility

Book of Runes

Girl's name	Rune symbols	Rune numbers	Total	Key number	Key word
Whitney	ᛈᚾᛁᛏᚻᛗᛊ	1033748	26	8	Dedication
Wilfrida	ᛈᛁᚾᚠᚱᛁᛋᚠ	13269313	28	1	Victory
Wilhelmina	ᛈᛁᚾᚾᛏᛗᛁᚻᚠ	1320422373	27	9	Accomplishment
Williamina	ᛈᛁᚾᚾᛗᛁᚻᚠ	1322332373	29	2	Friendship
Wilma	ᛈᛁᛗᛈᚠ	13223	11	2	Friendship
Winifred	ᛈᛁᚾᚠᚱᛗᛊ	13736941	34	7	Courage
Wynn	ᛈᛊᚻᚻ	1877	23	5	Caution
Xanthe	ᛈᚾᛏᚾᛗ	537304	22	4	Stability
Xaviera	ᚻᛈᛈᛁᛗᚱᚠ	5313493	28	1	Victory
Xena	ᛈᛗᚻᚠ	5473	19	1	Victory
Yasmin	ᛊᚠᛊᛈᚻᛁ	831237	24	6	Abundance
Yehuda	ᛊᛗᚾᚾᛊᚠ	840713	23	5	Caution
Yolanda	ᛊᛡᛈᚻᛊᛊᚠ	8423713	28	1	Victory
Yseult	ᛊᛊᛗᚻᛏ	814723	25	7	Courage
Yvette	ᛊᛈᛗᛏᛏᛗ	814334	23	5	Caution
Yvonne	ᛊᛈᛡᚻᛗ	814774	31	4	Stability
Zabrina	ᛉᚠᛒᚱᛁᚠ	4339373	32	5	Caution
Zara	ᛉᚱᚱᚠ	4393	19	1	Victory
Zelma	ᛉᛗᛏᛈᚠ	44223	15	6	Abundance
Zenobia	ᛉᛗᚻᛡᛒᛁᚠ	4474333	28	1	Victory
Zinnia	ᛉᛁᚻᚻᚠ	437733	27	9	Accomplishment
Zoë	ᛉᛡᛗ	444	12	3	Fertility
Zora	ᛉᛡᚱᚠ	4493	20	2	Friendship